MODERN GHOST STORIES

A MEDLEY OF

Dreams, Impressions and Spectral Illusions

MODERN GHOST STORIES

A MEDLEY OF

Dreams, Impressions and Spectral Illusions

BY

EMMA MAY BUCKINGHAM

Author of "A Self-Made Woman;" "Pearl, a Poem;" "The Silver Chalice," and "Parson Thorne's Trial, or His Second Love."

"There are more things in heaven and earth, Horatio, than are dreampt of in your philosophy."

WILDSIDE PRESS

COPYRIGHT BY
FOWLER & WELLS COMPANY,
1906.

TO
GERTRUDE T. VAUGHN,
IN MEMORY OF A HAPPY SUMMER AT
COLUMBIA UNIVERSITY, NEW YORK CITY,
THIS BOOK IS
AFFECTIONATELY DEDICATED BY
THE AUTHOR.

CONTENTS.

CHAPTER		PAGE
I.	Are We Naturally Superstitious?	5
II.	Was It a Spirit Telegram?	9
III.	What Was It?	14
IV.	Spectral Illusions	19
V.	The Spectral Hound	28
VI.	Was It a Spirit?	30
VII.	Who Was She?	32
VIII.	Psychological Impressions	42
IX.	How He Found His Ideal	51
X.	That Shadow in the Park	58
XI.	A Young Wife's Trial	60
XII.	Tongueless Voices	69
XIII.	The Weird Musician	75
XIV.	Irresistible Impulse	83
XV.	The Phantom Child	89
XVI.	A Dream Warning	95
XVII.	Dreams Fulfilled	100
XVIII.	A Vision of Heaven	110
XIX.	A Dream Over Bride Cake	114
XX.	The Haunted Chamber	116
XXI.	The Mystery of Riverford	124
XXII.	Elucidation	128

MODERN GHOST STORIES

BY

EMMA MAY BUCKINGHAM.

CHAPTER I.

ARE WE NATURALLY SUPERSTITIOUS?

THE wisest amongst us would probably be astonished at the number of tolerably well educated people who believe in prognostics, dreams, superstitions, old saws and "unlucky days." There are thousands of men and women, to-day, who think, as their grandmothers did a century ago, that it forebodes ill-luck to see the new moon over the left shoulder—that it is wrong to start on a journey or commence a new piece of work on Friday; while the majority of the people in our rural districts, learned and unlearned, place great stress upon the signs of the Zodiac. Their planting, sowing, grafting fruit trees, transplanting, weeding, reaping, mowing, pruning vines, and setting their fowls, must be done during certain phases of the moon—"when the sign is right." Mothers wean their babies, cut their children's hair, and pick their geese, only when the moon is new. Housewives boil soap, or plant flower and vegetable gardens, also, when the moon is in a certain quarter; while their husbands and brothers fish, shear sheep, and do a hundred other things, according to the sign-lore of their ancestors. Certain events occurring in the "old of the moon,"—such as births, are said, by the above-named class, to cause ill-luck. There are hundreds of intelligent people in our cities, as well as in the country, who will start and turn pale at the sound of the death watch or the howling of a dog—while tens of thousands believe that to dream of blood, of losing teeth, of crossing a muddy stream, of talking with, or, seeing friends who have long been dead, or absent, is a fore-runner of death, the loss of a friend, or, of certain disaster.

Others believe that to forget something and go back after it, is the sign of a fast coming accident; while fifty per cent. of our housekeepers see trouble looming up ahead of them whenever their bread cracks open in the middle, or a looking-glass is broken, or a picture falls from the wall; no matter how old or moth-eaten the cord may have been which had held it.

One of the most sensible old ladies I ever knew, in other things, was in the habit of saying: "My right eye-brow itches. There is a man coming here;" or, "My left eye-brow itches. Some women is coming to-day to see me." Or, "My ear rings dreadful loud. We shall hear of a death soon." She would say; "My nose itches—I shall be angry at someone before night;" and, "My left ear burns—somebody is talking about me!" And when I would laugh at the dear old soul, and try to reason her out of such nonsense, she would declare that she "never knew such signs to fail!"

Many intelligent people believe that it presages disaster to meet a hearse. They tell us that, "it is wrong to watch a friend out of sight, after one has said *good-bye*." An educated lady says: "Plants will not grow if you thank the donor for them; neither will seeds." A goodly number of the world's most enlightened inhabitants look with apprehension at an approaching comet;* for, according to the popular belief, comets have predicted war, plagues, and national troubles in all the ages of the past.

We know that astrology, witchcraft, sooth-saying and miracles are now considered exploded ideas—things of a past era—yet, there are many in our own land and times who say that people are possessed of good, as well as evil spirits. There are others who have faith in the charlatans who profess that they can pray fire out of burns, and "pow-wow" away diseases. Fortune-telling still lives in all civilized countries. We daily hear of *faith cures* and miraculous interventions, in spite of our boasted civilization.

The Chinese believe that the souls of the dead come back and partake of the good things which their surviving friends set out for them on holidays and anniversary occasions; while the army of spiritualists, with their mediums, seance seers, and "spiritual-clairvoyants," tell us that they hold communication with the spirits, of those who have departed from this earth-life, continually.

The murderer, who sees the ghosts of his victims; the engineer, who nightly imagines that the spirits of those whom he has killed, accidentally, appear to him, and the ghosts of unkind words to the dying, or, of lost opportunities to do good, are not the only shades that our poets sing about. One of the most intelligent writers of the nineteenth century said:

*Thousands of Europeans believe that the late comets and red-sunsets foretold the recent plagues, earthquakes, and the war in the Far East.

"There are more ghosts at table than the host's invited;" and it is true.

Many people believe in warnings, that is, in premonitions of death. They will tell you that they always hear unaccountable noises before the death of dear friends. We all know that, at times, the wisest and most skeptical among us approach very near the border-land of the unexplainable, if not supernatural. Mysterious sights and sounds and appearances, as well as experiences have occasionally defied reason herself and put our credulity to the hardest tests imaginable. Are we all more or less superstitious? Did not the great Napoleon Bonaparte believe in his "star of destiny," also, in "unlucky" and "lucky days?" The origin of "bad signs" dated back to antiquity.

The spilling of salt on the table is considered a very bad omen, because it is emblematic of friendship and hospitality; and spilling it is a sure sign of a quarrel, or disrupture of friendly relations. The seating of 13 at table is currently believed to be an omen of death to one of the guests, even in this twentieth century.

CHAPTER II.

WAS IT A SPIRIT TELEGRAM.

We hear a good deal about impressions nowadays, and the question which most interests one in regard to these psychological phenomena is not: what are they? but, *whence* are they? What causes these live thoughts, which, without any premonition, expectation, or desire on our part, take such instantaneous possession of our thoughts, that we find it impossible to shake them off, although like Banquo, we "bid them down"—thoughts that will rise again and again until some accident, or circumstance, or sudden death, tells us why our minds have been thus strangely agitated?

Is it instinct, this prescience, or soul-knowledge, this voiceless power, within, which moves us against our will, our reason or inclination; warns of danger ahead, bids us not take certain paths, or risks, or journeys? Do our good angels thus influence us through the medium of impressions? Or is it the Holy Spirit speaking to our consciousness—illumining our souls by sudden flashes of knowledge? Vain, vain are all these questions —yet how often have we been startled by the strange coincidence of friends, who are thousands of miles away, writing to us the very hour that we were writing to them? Where is the business man who has not been held back from some ruinous enterprise, or the traveler—or who has not been saved from some accident or a horrible death, by listening to and obeying this voiceless monitor—Impression?

Let us compare notes, Reader mine, and see who can send the greatest number of facts, real experiences of this kind, to the Phrenological Journal. I will begin, with the editor's permission, by an experience of my own, trusting that more interesting papers will follow from others on this subject.

In the spring of 1876 I was making an extensive tour of the Western States. In April, at the time of the great flood in the Mississippi river, I started from St. Louis, by steamboat, for St. Paul. It was then my intention to go to California, after visiting in uncle in Minnesota.

After we had gone some twenty-five miles up the river, the captain advised me to finish my journey "by rail," as the water was so high it was not considered safe for steamboats to pass under the bridges at Hannibal and St. Joseph. "Two boats were swamped last night," he added. I concluded that it would be as well to go back to Chicago and go directly to San Francisco from that point. I could visit St. Paul on my return.

On the 10th of May, I left the Revierre House, Chicago, for the railway station. I was impatient to begin my long anticipated journey to the Golden State, for which, I had given up a summer in Europe and the Centennial Exposition at Philadelphia. The morning was lovely. The time was Monday, 9 o'clock, I well remember. When about half-way to Lake station, something seemed to say to me: "You must go home!" Now, I had at that moment, no more intention of going East than I had of taking a balloon to the moon; so, I said to my unwelcome thought: "I will not go home! I am bound for the

Golden Gate before I stop." "But you *must* go home, you are greatly needed there!" I stopped short,—for I was just entering the ladies' waiting-room,—and wondered what it all meant? "Am I asleep and dreaming, or homesick? Or, is my mind a little bewildered by this anticipated vacation?" I asked myself. They were all well at my home, when they wrote last, I was free to go where I wished. There was no reason, as far as I could judge, for my return home before my purpose was accomplished; but the impression was fast becoming an imperative fixed idea. The thought that I was needed for some purpose grew, in a few moments, to a necessity—a strong conviction. "This must be an acute fit of home-sickness—the first attack I ever experienced," I added nervously, "but I never felt such an irresistible desire to see my home and friends as I do at this moment. What *does* it *mean?*" I looked at my watch. The Western train would be due in ten minutes. I paced the waiting-room in an agony of impatience. Reason, desire for sight-seeing, interest, inclination, were all at war with this stern command, which had taken possession of my soul, and were soon merged into one voiceless longing for home, for a word with the dear ones there, who had bidden me "Godspeed" so unselfishly six months before. Oh, yes, strange and unaccountable as it still seems to me, I took a ticket for Philadelphia, instead of San Francisco. As the early train had gone, we did not start till 3 P.M. I telegraphed. No reply.* We traveled all night. During the long, wakeful hours, I had but one thought,

---

*I tried to telegraph them that I was coming, but received no reply in time for the Western train, as my home was then in the country, five miles from the nearest telegraph office.

one feeling, namely, that of impatient longing to be at home. The following day was also spent in ceaseless worry. The cars seemed to crawl. The minutes were like so many hours. When we reached Suspension Bridge on Tuesday afternoon, I was too ill with a headache to think of traveling further that night, and, to my dismay, was obliged to remain at the Falls until the following day, but anxiety drove sleep from my pillow. The certainty that something terrible had happened, or, was going to happen, had, by this time, taken full possession of my mind. I knew that the TO BE, was something that HAD BEEN; I grieved over the impending calamity in silence, without even guessing what it was, until Wednesday morning.* About 10 o'clock, A.M., while sitting in Prospect Park, my eyes fixed on the magnificent falls, my thoughts in one mad whirl of conjecture, my anxiety as suddenly left me as it had come. I felt such a relief from the depression which had controlled both mind and action for the past forty-eight hours, that, I laughed and sang to myself. The trouble was all gone, and with it, my hurry to go on my journey. I could have shouted aloud, for very joy, so great was the rebound of my spirits after such a season of unnatural agitation.

As I stepped from the train at the station nearest my home, a friend met me and said: "Your brother was buried this morning at 10 o'clock. He died on Monday at 9 o'clock in the morning."

I was not at all surprised at this. He was dying at the very moment the impression first came to me that I was wanted at

---

*Of course they had telegraphed, but as I had left St. Louis, I did not receive the message.

home. They had buried him on Wednesday, when the worry left my mind so suddenly—just laid him in the grave! Truly, there was, then, no further need of hurrying eastward. I was too late to look into his dying eyes, to hold his dying hand, to see his dear, dead face. He was gone from my home—from my sight forever in this life!

Now, the question arises: What was it? Did his desire to see me, when spirit and body were parting, added to the wish of other members of my family for my presence, send a resistless brain-wave or spirit telegram to me, a distance of over a thousand miles? *Did* his longing to see or speak to me, then, create a sort of invisible, intangible telephonic communication with my mind, or did his spirit actually fly to me at the moment of its release from the body? If all these questions are vain, unanswerable, I must still ask: "What swift messenger communicated to my consciousness the above-named premonition of sickness and bereavement? An impending sorrow, so intense, that I dared not ask, by telegram, its nature, yet a trouble I did not guess correctly, or know for a certainty, until I reached my destination. Who sent that spirit telegram while he was dying of heart failure?

> Oh, learned students in psychology,
> Or, sage philosophers, pray, answer me.

CHAPTER III.

WHAT WAS IT?

IN my last paper for your Journal, I stated that some voiceless, invisible monitor so strongly impressed my mind with the idea that I was needed at home, that I was compelled against my will and better judgment to retrace my steps a thousand or more miles eastward—although at the time westward bound—that I reached home too late to see my brother or attend his funeral. I found soon after my return, however, why I had been so greatly needed at home. My father was not only crushed with grief at the loss of his eldest son, but was, himself, slowly dying with an incurable disease. He had been ill all winter, but, as no immediate danger was apprehended, my friends did not like to spoil my visit by the above information. He was a great sufferer during the last months of his life, not only in body, but in mind. I think, now, that he must have been affected with melancholia, that his reason was, at times, so greatly clouded that his thoughts wandered in the mazes of delirium. He thoroughly understood the fatal nature of his disease—knew that he must soon face the realities of an unknown state of existence; and the burden of his cry was, "I have 'sinned away the day of grace.' There is no pardon for me, or peace either in this world or in the life to come! I shall be a lost soul, lost in the perdition described by the Bible, lost through all the eternities!"

It was impossible to console him or turn his thoughts from this theme for any length of time, and I would find him on his knees, pleading with God for pardon, for peace; his face wearing the most sorrowful expression; but no answer came to still the tempest of anguish within his soul.

A few days before his death, he said, "I have given up all—I have cast my trembling soul upon God's mercy—Can I do more?" I said: "Nothing except to take Christ at his word and trust in his loving kindness and tender mercy." His death was peaceful, thank God! If anything could have comforted us after the weary soul had taken its departure from his wasted body, the peaceful expression of his dying eyes—the sweet, majestic smile which was frozen upon his dead face, should have reassured us,—indeed, did confirm my belief that a just and all-merciful Saviour had heard his prayers and given sweet peace and rest, at last, to his tempest-tossed spirit.

I was so worn out with watching,—for he had seemed to cling to me—refusing other attendants all through the last weeks of his life—that I was compelled to seek a few hours' sleep the night after he died; but the thought of leaving his beloved clay alone, for the first time, seemed so unnatural, that I could not sleep for weeping. At length, the remembrance of his dying moments, with the great calm which had settled on his features, convinced me that his spirit was free from doubt and suffering—from sorrow and death. But soon, a great and uncontrollable desire to see him once more, if but for a moment, and ask him what and where and how he was, took entire possession of my mind. I realized, then, the full meaning of Tennyson's lines in his sweet poem entitled "Maude," namely:

> "Ah, Christ! that it were possible
> For one short hour to see
> The souls we loved, that they might tell us
> What and where they be?"

About 3 o'clock in the morning, the sound of wheels outside informed me that a married sister, who was expected, had arrived. She came directly to my chamber and sat down on the side of my bed. We talked for, perhaps, half an hour, when she went downstairs. I was, I remember, very wide-awake by that time. Dawn was just breaking. I could distinctly see the outlines of the furniture in my chamber. I recollect exactly how the room and everything looked; how a pearl-colored stream of light quivered through the blinds and rested upon the carpet —how the shadows seemed to shrink away and hover darkly in the corner, as if loth to be driven out by the advancing day. It was a low ceilinged room under the eaves. The windows were very small and narrow. At that early hour, at least one-half of my chamber was still wrapped in a shadowy twilight gloom. The only article of furniture opposite my bed, was a small table, upon which stood a large vase of waxen flowers covered by a glass shade. I was watching the growing dawn and curiously noting the colorless appearance of the flowers, which, by daylight, rivaled the rainbow in brilliant coloring, for the shape of the bouquet as well as that of both vase and table were perfectly visible. I remember, that, even while looking at the flowers, I was conscious of my great loss, so true it is that one's eyes and thoughts may be occupied by different things at the same time, but I had not once thought of *fear* of anything supernatural in connection with my dead father, whose remains I had a few hours before seen lying so still and rigid with the seal of *silence* upon the beloved features. I have been intentionally explicit and, I fear, prolix, in describing my state of mind and the appearance of my chamber, in order to prove to you that I was wide-awake at that time. I had spoken of the peaceful expression which had settled on the face so soon to be hidden forever from our sight, to my sister whose arrival and conversation had somewhat comforted me, and I might have followed my recent habit of falling asleep at daylight after a sleepless night, had not a sudden apparition driven me from my bed and sent me shrieking down the stairs. I had been, as I told you, wide-awake—looking at the colorless appearance of the artificial flowers near the wall, when I suddenly knew that something stirred amid the shadows of the dimly lighted room. At the same instant the figure of a man in a crouching position appeared close to the wall opposite my bed. It seemed to be alive and moved its right hand across its face as if in an agony of facial pain. I sprang up in bed, looked again, and recognized the form and features of my *dead father*. He was looking intently at me, as if trying to speak, yet I heard no voice; but O, the intense agony depicted on his face, I shall never, *never* forget! It was an expression which only the eternally damned might wear—the anguish of a lost spirit was painted in that one wordless glance! It was then that I realized the meaning of *fear*. Was he coming toward me? What were his burning, wide open, horrified eyes trying to tell me? I could not tell, but like a mad woman, rushed down the stairs; and, they all said I had been dreaming. Without waiting to explain the cause of my alarm, I went immediately to the room where I had seen my father's dead body lying so still, and, of course, found his lifeless form just as I had left it, on the previous night—only the face and hand seemed colder, more like marble than flesh. Then, urged by my friends, I told what I had seen, when, in order to soothe my perturbed feelings, they made me follow them back to my chamber and tried to convince me that there had been nothing there except the flower-stand—that I had only been dreaming. "Ah, but I saw the flowers and table at the same time," I answered, "I know I have not been asleep." "Oh, yes, you have," they persisted. I had not, however, but *what was it?*

Why was the vision sent? But I yet do not believe it was to tell me that his fears had become a reality, because "Whosoever will may come and partake of the waters of life freely." He *tried* to come, Oh, so tearfully, so prayerfully!

But *what* did I see?

Do you answer: "It was only a picture of the imagination, an hallucination, the reaction of over-wrought nerves and brain?" Or, do you say: "It was your father's long illness, coupled with his diseased imagination and your own painful anxiety painted upon the camera of your mind, which appeared to you instead of the spirit or shade of your father?"

This appears like a sensible solution to the mystery, for I went with him in spirit into the cloud and into the valley of the shadow, and my brain was naturally filled with mournful pictures of his living suffering face, instead of the placid features of the dead —a picture too new and strangely, majestically beautiful to be at that hour photographed upon my mind. I have never been a believer in supernatural appearances, in ghosts, or hobgoblins, or the so-called belief in spiritual manifestations, or spiritual clairvoyance, although, I have always been cognizant of the fact that we have all more or less superstition in our nature. I have all these years been trying to make myself believe that it was a morning dream, a picture of an overtaxed fancy—yet, in moments of depression, the thought comes home to me, that, he might have come back for a moment, or that he lingered a few hours, just to show me that his spirit was lost—and, for the time being, it is all so terribly real, that reason and philosophy are submerged by a tidal wave of wordless agony. Yet dreams between sleeping and waking are so real, that it is hard to distinguish them from waking visions; and I ask vainly: What was it?

CHAPTER IV.

SPECTRAL ILLUSIONS.

WISHING to ascertain whether any of my relatives and acquaintances ever experienced anything of the kind, either before or after the death of a near friend, I called on a neighbor, who had recently lost her father, and, in the course of our conversation, asked if she had ever had any warning of his death? Her reply was,

"No, but my brother and sister out West had, and, really, something very peculiar happened to my father just before he died. I was with him at the time, and noticed that his mind appeared to wander; for he seemed in a manner absent from the body. I thought it best to arouse him, when he opened his eyes with a sigh, and asked regretfully:

"Why did you call me back so soon? I have just been out West to see the children. Jack was out in his wheat field harrowing in his grain with a 'brush' (the top of a tree, you know), for a harrow. The 'brush' was drawn by two milk white horses. His gun was leaning against a small tree. I didn't stop to speak to him, for he was only a short distance from me and was going, like myself, toward his house. I went in, and saw George and daughter Madge. Madge was sick on the bed, but before I could speak to her, for I had just reached the foot of her bed, you called me back." Father died soon after this, but the first letter we received from this brother and sister out West, was written on the very day father died—about the same hour (Western time) of his dream-visit to them. It read as follows:—"I write in haste, because we are very anxious to hear from father. Jack was out in the wheat fields to-day, about 2 o'clock, harrowing in his wheat, and, all at once, thought he saw father coming hastily toward him, looking as natural as life. He could not have helped seeing Jack if he had been flesh and blood, for Jack was going directly toward him with our white horses and was only a few rods away. He seemed to be looking at Jack, too. Seeing father seem to hesitate, then turn and go into the house, Jack unhitched the 'brush,' tied his horses to the tree where his gun stood, took the gun, and followed him into the house. Judge of his surprise at finding no one here, except George and myself. I was very sick that day, unable to get up, and Jack had promised to shoot a duck or prairie chicken for me. As he came in, I asked him what he had done with his game? He replied, 'I forgot it, Madge; I was in such a hurry to see father. Where is he?' Then I told him that I just had a terrible fright—that I had seen father come in and stand at the foot of my bed, then instantly disappear *without opening the door.* Jack turned as white as a ghost, and said, 'I was sure I saw him come into this house. One of us is going to die, Madge.' Now, do write, or telegraph at *once,* for we are sure father is sick or dead. Madge.'"

"On comparing notes," continued my informant, "we found that father's apparition had appeared to Jack and Madge *the same day and hour* he had told me that *he saw them* in their western home *fifteen hundred miles* away." If my friend had been an imaginative woman, or one given to spectral illusions, or a spiritualist, or professional clairvoyant, I should not have wondered so much at her statement, or her sister's, but she is a clear-eyed, sensible, hard-working mother of several children—with no time for reading, or, idle dreaming; much less, of psychological research into the realm of metaphysics.

Still, it has puzzled me a good deal to account for the apparent fact of her father's *mind* being absent from the body long enough to go so great a distance, then return to it in an instant; secondly, to understand why his children's minds or clairvoyant perceptions were so wrought upon, that they were able to perceive him at the same moment (making allowance for Western time) that he thought he saw them.

Another lady friend, a member of one of our orthodox churches, and a firm believer in the doctrine of "Holiness" or "Christian Perfection," said to me a few months ago: "I always have a warning before the death of near friends. Let me tell you one or two of my singular experiences.

"About three years ago, while I was lying down to rest, early in the afternoon, I seemed to see before me a coffin in which a small woman was lying. I was wideawake at the time, and, as the illusion faded away, wondered if I were going to be ill or insane. Then a funeral procession seemed to be passing, but there were very few mourners. I sprang from my couch, and, feeling afraid of myself, went downstairs. I was so weak with fright—for both pictures were very real—that I could scarcely move. Word came *that same day* that my sister Delilah was dead. On the day of her funeral the snow was so deep that very few people, except her own family, were present. Delilah was very small, always, but she looked so like the woman I had seen in my vision that I came very near fainting when I saw her in the coffin."

Do you think that such visions, as you call them, are common to all people?" I asked.

"No, indeed; only to certain individuals. I think my answer is correct, for I have taken pains to question a large number of people, and find that perhaps not more than one in a hundred have such vivid clairvoyant impressions. One of my lady friends has had a similar experience. She often addresses the young people during our extra religious meetings. Once, last winter, in the midst of an earnest exhortation, she cried, excitedly, 'I see, I see a coffin!' then sank fainting to the floor. At the close of the service she said to the minister, 'Something is the matter at my sister's. I must go there, a distance of twelve miles,' she added, 'immediately.'

"He told her that she was only nervous, and advised her not to start before daybreak. She took his advice, but spent a sleepless night. In the morning a messenger came from her sister's with bad news. Her nephew had been struck by a train whilst endeavoring to cross the railroad on his return from church and was instantly killed, about *the time of her vision.* His remains had to be shoveled into a box. Another experience. Once my little son stood before me with an agonized expression. I knew he was at school, a few rods distant, at that moment—knew that I had not seen my little boy weeping before me, but was so impressed by the vision that I ran all the way to the village schoolhouse, where I was not surprised to find his inhuman teacher, a fiend in the semblance of a young lady, treating him cruelly. One glance at his little, tear-stained face, his quivering lips, as a heavy blow from a ruler fell upon his extended hand, was enough. I sprang forward and caught the poor child in my arms and carried him into the open air, too late, however, to avert the terrible convulsion which seized him as the natural result of such chastisement. He had been a delicate child from his birth—was then but 6 years old—I believe my interference saved his life. Frank did not recover from that nervous shock for years. The teacher informed me, subsequently, that she had unwittingly *punished the wrong boy.* Some one had hit her in the face with a paper ball, she said, and it made her very angry. Her cruelty made her unpopular, I presume, yet it was a small offence for such heroic treatment. Another boy confessed to flinging the ball at her face, but declared that he 'only meant to have a little fun. It was such sport to see the school ma'am angry.' I wondered at the time how my bashful little Frank could do such a thing."

These visions and impressions, or clairvoyant perceptions, are not confined to women. A lawyer of talent and culture told me the following circumstance: "I was considerably startled one night in my study by seeing my brother-in-law, John Fell, standing beside me, with both of his limbs cut off at the knee. He was bleeding profusely and seemed to be suffering great pain and about to fall. I put out my hand to save him, when the illusion disappeared and I was alone. I had often had a sort of *second sight,* or forewarning, of coming disaster, and knew that I should soon hear bad news from my native county, a hundred miles distant, where he resided. It was useless to reason or philosophize. I was as certain that trouble was ahead as I was that I was alive. My wife laughed at me and said that I was studying too hard—that I ought to take a vacation trip. I could not sleep, but spent the night in a sort of listening stupor. At about 5 o'clock the next morning there was a hasty ringing of the door bell. I was up and dressed, as I had for several hours been listening for that very sound. When I opened the door I knew what was coming before the messenger delivered his message. 'There is a man down at the railway crossing who was run over by the night train, a stranger to us all. He says you will know him. That's all he said—both of his legs are broken.'

"'That man's name is Fell!' I exclaimed. It was true. He had the day before obtained a situation on the night train between this city and Harrisburg, without my knowledge. When we had last heard from him he was at work on his farm, as I have said, a hundred miles distant. I am willing to swear to this statement. Besides this, I have had similar experiences, yet seldom speak of them for fear that I shall be misunderstood by my most intimate friends. The poor fellow was brought to my house and remained there until he was able to be taken to his home. He told me that the moment he was struck that he instantly thought of me and seemed to see me in my office writing. My wife does not laugh now at my impressions." I have known John Fell for years and know the above statement is true. John Fell is a cripple and the last time I saw him was walking by the aid of crutches. He corroborated the above story.

Ammie C. Cheever, a native of Boston, lived alone in his farmhouse at Milford, Pa. His aged mother, who resided in Boston, often predicted that some harm would befall him. One morning in October, 1883, she suddenly exclaimed, "Ammie is murdered! I see my dear son lying before me with a bullet through his head."

In vain her friends endeavored to pacify her, but she continued at intervals during the day to say that her son was surely dead. A dispatch was received the next morning stating that Ammie C. Cheever, of Milford, had just been found dead in the vicinity of his home which soon corroborated his mother's fears. John F. Greening has since been found guilty of the murder and sentenced to the Eastern Penitentiary, Pa., for a term of seven years.

Could Mrs. Cheever have been dreaming? If so, what caused her to dream at the very hour of the murder?

Spectral illusions and clairvoyant perceptions have been common in all ages and climes and peoples, as has been already stated.

Do the dying see angels from the unseen world? Are they gifted with clearer vision when about to join the pale army of the dead?

I heard a clergyman tell the following incident only a few days since: "A little child was dying. Suddenly it smiled exultingly. A lady bent over its cradle, when the little one frowned, as if something had intercepted its vision. The lady stepped back, when instantly the smile returned to the infant's dying face and lingered there until death came. What did the little one see? Are we nearer to the other world than we dream, and are the spirits of the 'just made perfect' all around us? Who can answer?"

A lady friend who had long been ill was dying. A few months earlier she had lost a beautiful little boy named George—her only child. His death seemed to wean my friend from the earth. A few minutes before she departed she smiled joyously and stretched out her arms, crying out: "I see Georgie! My little Georgie!"

A violent paroxysm of coughing ensued and death soon came to her relief. *Did* she see her lost boy? *Was* he sent to welcome his mother to her new home beyond the waves of time? Ah, who can tell?

Once I heard a dying man say:

"This room is full of spirits. Why did you call me? I saw all of my old neighbors—men and women who have been dead many a year."

A near relative says: "Just before my little Edith died I saw her standing at the head of the chamber stairs, draped in white. Thinking she was walking in her sleep, I ran upstairs, but when I reached the landing she disappeared. I rushed frantically to her room and found my darling fast asleep in bed. She died very suddenly a few days afterward. Just before she breathed her last she said: "Oh, mother, see those pretty little children there—and hear their sweet singing. *Don't* you hear them?" What *did* the dying child see? Were the *children* angels? *Did* she hear them sing? Ah, who knows? Who knows?

For several weeks before the death of my aged mother she called me almost nightly and said: "Your father has just been here. He always smiles and asks, 'How are you?' or, 'Are you well, Mahala?'" She was about ninety-six years old when she died, but her mind was unimpaired. *Did* she see him? Was he permitted to visit her?

A young lady whom I well knew in her girlhood and early womanhood had an unpleasant habit of amusing herself by teasing her little motherless nephew. One summer evening, while sitting in her front yard, she suddenly saw the boy's dead mother fluttering in the air just above her head, reaching out her hands as if attempting to seize the young lady, who ran screaming into the house and fainted upon the threshold. She has never fully recovered from the shock and for many years has been a nervous wreck. But the warning was not sent in vain, for she was kinder to the orphan after that experience. It is useless to reason with her on the subject, for she will believe to her dying day that her sister's ghost appeared to her. *Did* she see it, or was it a sudden fit of insanity? Or was it a dream? Did she lose outward consciousness for a few seconds and see the reproduction of her dead sister's face and form, or was it some picture seen in childhood which had been long hidden away on some lower shelf of memory until suddenly recalled by some association of ideas?

However, the warning caused by the appearance of the wraith proved effectual.

CHAPTER V.

THE SPECTRAL HOUND.

THE following story is as true as the Gospel. Several years ago, while sojourning with my invalid mother in a hamlet in Northeastern-Pennsylvania, during an epidemic of *la grippe,* when there were not enough well people to take care of the sick, I had a curious experience.

For eight nights I had watched beside my mother's couch without sleeping as many hours. On the night in question my mother was so ill that her physician declared she would not live till daybreak, but she had fallen into a restful sleep about 1 o'clock in the morning and I ventured to leave her room in order to get some much-needed refreshment.

I found a good fire in the kitchen range, made a cup of coffee and went into the pantry for a dish of batter, thinking that some warm buckwheat cakes with butter and honey could be quickly prepared. As I came out of the pantry, which opened into the kitchen, judge of my surprise on seeing a large, black hound standing in front of me, snarling silently and showing his white teeth, as if disputing my passage. I saw him as plainly as I see this paper, and recognized him as my girl friend Kathryn's pet dog. Thinking that his mistress had entered the house quietly, I cried: "Kathryn! *how* did you and Major get in? I thought the doors were all locked!" There was no answer. I looked down at the dog and saw him slowly waste away before my eyes until only a skeleton remained. Then, for the first time since I had beheld the apparition I was so beside myself with fright that the earthen bowl fell from my hand and was shattered into a hundred fragments, and, of course, spilled its contents.

The noise awoke my mother and I heard her labored breathing. The ribs of the skeleton faded away as I sprang past it and entered the sick room, where I found the dear invalid struggling for breath. She had slept too long, and but for my sudden fright would have strangled to death in all probability. But the crisis had passed. In my effort to resuscitate her my courage returned and I said to myself, "Pshaw! It was only a spectral illusion!" then went to the kitchen, but there where the dream-hound had stood were the fragments of earthenware and a pool of creamy batter; but the outside doors of our cottage were all locked securely.

Even horses, cats and dogs are often terrified by things which to us are invisible. What do they see?

CHAPTER VI.

WAS IT A SPIRIT?

ANOTHER true story, for the truth of which I am willing to vouch for under oath before a hundred people.

A year or two after my dear and honored mother left me alone in the homestead I received a large sum of money, the payment of a loan, late one Saturday afternoon, and, as there was not a bank within twenty miles, slipped the roll of bills and checks into my pocket with serious misgivings, because some tramps had been seen prowling around the neighborhood. After the man who had paid me had left the house I sat down to my supper, poured a cup of coffee and put some food upon my plate, when I suddenly became aware that there was some one in the room, and hastily looked toward the door, at my right, which led into the hall. Imagine my surprise on seeing a woman, whom I did not recognize at first, standing between my chair and the door above mentioned. She appeared to be enveloped in a cloud of gray mist, but her white face, with its brilliant eyes, was distinctly visible. She seemed to be looking at me intently, and I wondered why she did not speak, for I thought she was a neighbor, and asked:

"How in the world did you get in?" She did not answer, and, knowing that the outside doors were securely locked, I began to feel a little nervous, but asked her to be seated. She did not stir. Then I said to myself, "It is a shadow—my own shade," and laughed to keep up my courage. But at that moment I happened to turn my eyes toward the wall ahead of me and saw my own shadow sharply defined against it, and remembered that the lamp was on a table behind me. Without moving my head I turned my eyes again to the right. The figure was still there, and I *knew* that it was not my reflection, and sprang from my chair as the truth slowly burned itself upon my inner consciousness that the apparition was nothing of flesh and blood, but the shade of my dear, *dead mother!* (But was it? Who can tell?)

Something like the shock of an electric battery held me powerless for a moment, then the figure slowly faded into nothingness! I rushed from the room and house, and told my nearest neighbor what I had seen.

She simply laughed and said: "Why, you were napping. You did not see a single thing!" Later in the evening, after my nervous fright had subsided, I returned to my home, but the sight of my untasted supper did not reassure me, but rather convinced me that I had really *seen an apparition.* "Oh, no, simply a spectral illusion," I concluded, and, with a strong effort of will power, banished the incident from my mind.

The following evening I attended church, but carried my valuable papers, bank books and money with me, for the first time since my bereavement. Imagine my surprise, on reaching home, to find the door which I had carefully locked *wide open!* The lock had been broken and the house searched by burglars, but the valuables which they had sought—except a gold watch and some silverware which I had securely hidden—were safe in my pocket.

Now, what of spectral illusions as warnings? Will you censure me, kind reader, if I tell you that I shall believe, till my dying day, that the shade of my sainted mother appeared to me as a warning?

Perhaps my guardian angel wanted to put me on my guard, knowing that an attempt to rob or murder me would be made on the following evening if I remained at home; or, if absent, to burglarize the homestead. If it was simply an imaginary wraith or brain picture, it probably saved my life and money.

CHAPTER VII.

WHO WAS SHE?

In the summer of 1884 Broad Mountain House had a pleasant addition to its boarders. The new arrivals were from Philadelphia and consisted of the following-named ladies and gentlemen: Mr. and Mrs. Welcome Gaye, their sister-in-law, Mrs. William Gaye a widow and her two daughters, Katherine, a maiden lady of thirty, perhaps, and Eulalie, a beautiful blonde of eighteen, just out of boarding school; Lieut. Charles Gaye, their brother, and his friend, Col. John Wolfington, of the same city. I have been intentionally explicit in describing this party of summer boarders for reasons that the reader will understand later.

Mrs. Gaye, the widow, was an invalid. She was always complaining of her ailments, but declared that their visit to the mountains was more for her daughter, Eulalie's, health than for her own. Eulalie's lungs had been weak since an attack of pneumonia the previous winter. She was engaged to be married to Col. Wolfington in the coming autumn. It was natural that the mother should desire, above all things else, that her daughter's health should be re-established before leaving the maternal roof, "for she is my favorite child," added the garrulous old lady.

Katherine Gaye was a college graduate, and, as Mrs. Welcome Gaye said, "a very strong-minded young woman." I was young then, and felt like studying her from a distance, but soon found that she was, as she boasted, "a perfect bundle of good health, without any troublesome nerves," to prevent her from enjoying life. She often declared that she was "not the possessor of any isms," and laughed at believers of mesmerism, magnetism, spiritualism, etc. They could all be psychologically explained, she said.

Although her favorite study was psychology, she was very fond of natural history—read Lyell, Cuvier, Audubon, Huxley and Darwin with her brother. She had folios of birds, insects, mosses, plants, ferns and wild flowers; and not only walked several miles each day in search of such treasures, but spent many hours in arranging her specimens while her brother read aloud their favorite authors. She interested me greatly in Nature study, for which I am still grateful.

Miss Eula Gaye was her Aunt Welcome Gaye's favorite. She spent much time with her aunt, whose rooms adjoined mine, and we soon became very good friends and were much together during the summer. Eula's health did not allow her to take long walks like her brother and sister, but she was very fond of the beautiful mosses, the upright and trailing ferns which grew in such wild luxuriance upon Broad Mountain. She would sit for hours arranging her vines and mosses in hanging baskets and filling her miniature grotto and fernery.

"They must not die. I have no taste for dried, dead specimens like Katha," she often said. "I want all of my plants and pets to be alive. I love to see them grow. I like to have everything thrive and enjoy life."

One day I found her crying pitifully over some dead ferns which she had transplanted. "I wanted them to get rooted, for they are to grace my new home next winter," she said, a pink blush staining her usually white cheeks. "But, oh, how sorry I shall be to leave this dear mountain! I wish I could take it all home with me!" Then, with a little sigh, "I am so tired of the city, where I was so cruelly ill all last winter, that, were it not for *somebody* who would miss me too much I would remain here all winter."

I have never seen a more delicate, flower-like face, or a more sensitive, lovable girl than Eulalie Gaye. Her mind was purity itself, her thoughts and words crystallized music and poetry. She was so careful of other people's feelings, so fearful of giving offence or trouble, even to the servants, that it was not possible to help loving the gentle, affectionate Eulalie, whose greatest charm was her unconsciousness of her own worth and loveliness and wealth and station in social circles. Why, she treated me, a hard-working teacher and writer, like an equal; and I do not believe that she ever noticed that I wore cotton prints and cheap muslins, while she was attired in Paris-made gowns of silk or India muslins, with lovely imported lace and embroidery trimmings.

Toward the latter part of September Eula grew a little tired of the mountains. The fading, changing foliage affected her spirits so greatly that her friends felt obliged to hurry her off to Cape May.

We soon learned that the sea air seemed to restore her spirits, that her languor and hectic fever decreased daily, and that her cough was better; then, that her lover agreed with her physician in thinking that a sea voyage and winter spent in the South of France would completely restore the health of the beloved invalid. They returned to the city, and, having obtained her mother's consent to an immediate marriage, preparations for the wedding were soon completed, state rooms engaged for them on an outgoing steamer, and friends invited to witness a ceremony destined never to be consummated.

A letter lies before me now, giving a description of her wedding gifts, which she wrote, "are pouring in upon me like a gold and silver shower. The Colonel's present is a complete set of pearls. Ann is continually answering the door bell, and I am so tired that I can only lie back in my easy chair and look at the beautiful presents, while Katha reads the cards and notes which accompanied them. We sail to-morrow, immediately after the wedding breakfast."

Poor Eulalie! Over-fatigue and excitement caused a violent fit of coughing that night and a severe hemorrhage of the lungs followed. Of course, the marriage was postponed and a fortnight later Eulalie Gaye, in her wedding robes, was lying in her casket, the bride of *Death*. The bereaved young bridegroom followed her to her grave with the other mourners, and thus ended my beloved friend's earth-life. The next letter was from her sister Katherine, giving a description of Eula's last sickness. "It was the most agonizing death scene I ever witnessed," she wrote. "Eula wept continually for days and begged us not to let her die. When Col. Wolfington came to see her she sobbed aloud and cried, 'Surely *you* will not let me die! I am too young to go out *alone* into the darkness—and the loathsome grave—away from you all! I can not, I *must not* die! Doctor, can you not save me? John, hold me back from death—dear John—' Another hemorrhage followed, and she never spoke again. John Wolfington had to be led, almost carried, from the chamber. Even after death, Eula's face, once so smiling and sweetly placid, looked as if her grief at leaving us all was stamped upon it. Her last moments were spent in looking at each one of us with wide-open, terror-stricken eyes, as if appealing to us for help. Alas! *love* even, could not hold her back from the clutch of Death's relentless fingers! Mother's nerves are so shattered by Eula's sudden death that we have decided to close our house and go abroad for the coming winter. Everything here reminds us of our loss. It makes me rebellious to think that her mosses, the delicate ferns in her window garden, her pet birds and tiny goldfish are all alive, while their mistress, our beautiful Eulalie, is, even now, moldering away in the grave. There is—there *must* be another life beyond this incomplete existence."

Now, my incredulous reader, here comes the strangest part of my story. The following summer the widow Gaye, her daughter Katherine and son, Lieut. Gaye, again visited the Mountain House, where I still boarded. Mr. and Mrs. Welcome came later. Lieut. Gaye did not appear to be sensitive or imaginative, but rather the reverse. He talked a good deal about materialism; said that the organ or spirituality was a myth. He had, he affirmed, convinced himself that death ended everything; that *memory,* at least, died with the body, because it was also material. He said that he had built breastworks of the dead bodies of soldiers with as steady nerves as if handling logs or stones. Report spoke of him as an officer whose narrow escapes and heroic daring proved that he was not wanting in courage while doing service in the frontiers. Judge of my astonishment on hearing him and Miss Gaye relate the following singular experience one evening while we were in their aunt's private parlor:

Miss Katherine was giving her reasons for not returning to their old home in Philadelphia, for they had not resided there since Eulalia's death. She said: "After we were all ready to leave the house last fall, and the servants had been discharged, I left mother waiting for the carriage and ran upstairs to pack away some linen just returned from the laundry. It had belonged to sister Eula, and I wanted to lock it up in the clothes press in one of her rooms.

"Without the least thought of fear or superstition, I went hastily into her little parlor. You know how that suite of rooms is situated, Charles?"

" 'Yes.' The rooms are in the second story, and the outside shutters and windows were all securely fastened," she added, as she handed me the diagram, showing that the parlor, chamber, dressing room and closets all communicated—that there was no way of egress except through the parlor door into the upper corridor. After I had examined the diagram and handed it to Lieut. Gaye, Miss Katherine continued:

"You can judge of my astonishment on seeing in Eula's little parlor a young and lovely girl. She appeared to be wringing her hands and weeping silently. In the dim light I did not at first recognize her, thought: 'It is either a pretty shoplifter or one of the maids who has returned after some forgotten article or to fasten the windows.' I followed her into the bedroom. She stopped at the foot of the bed upon which my sister died, and, still weeping convulsively, turned her agonized face toward me, oh, so pleadingly; but there was no sound. Then I recognized her. Aunt, it was my dead sister Eulalie!

"I shall never forget the sorrowful expression of her death-white face! I sprang toward her, but she eluded my grasp, then, like a noiseless shadow, passed into her old dressing-room, and *disappeared*. I was still in full possession of my senses. 'Some one is playing on my credulity—trying to frighten me,' I said, aloud, as I set my basket of linen down and followed her. The dressing-room was empty, so was the dark closet. I looked behind the doors, under the shelves of the wardrobe and closet, tried the windows and shutters, looked under the bed, everywhere, but without success. Hastily locking all of the doors, I went downstairs, feeling sure that I had seen Eula's *spirit*. You may imagine how my flesh seemed to creep—how difficult it was to act in mother's presence as if nothing strange had happened, as I hurried her into the carriage that was to convey us to the station. This is the first time I have mentioned the occurrence, but I came near telling my brother when he asked why we did not go to our own home instead of wandering around in this aimless manner. But nothing on earth will convince me that I did not see Eulalie's apparition, and this thought has caused my delay in urging mother to return with me to the dear old home."

Then Lieut. Gaye related his experience. He had not dared to write it, on account of his mother's weak nerves, but as this was a conference meeting, perhaps an exchange of experiences might be well. I will give his own version.

"I visited Philadelphia some three months after our house was closed, and, more out of idle curiosity than anything else, used my night key and made a tour of the lower rooms, then started for my old chamber and study on the second floor. Before I had ascended three steps I saw that I was not alone. A young girl, whose gait and form reminded me of sister Eulalie, was about five steps from the head of the stairs.

"Thinking it must be one of our former maids who had been left as caretaker of the house, I did not hasten, but soon lost sight of her in the corridor.

"After I had gone through my old rooms and Katherine's I unlocked the door leading to Eulalie's parlor and stood for a moment looking at the pretty, familiar apartment, and thinking of its late occupant. You know I was not able to attend the funeral, and did not see her after I left here last summer.

"Suddenly, like a flashlight on my consciousness, came the conviction that I was again near the young girl who had preceded me up the stairs. She was just going into the bedroom, where, they told me, Eulalie breathed her last. I locked the hall door and the one leading into her bed-chamber, then approached the girl, saying: 'Now, my lady, I have caught you. What are you doing here?'

"She was leaning over the bed, weeping silently and wringing her hands. I put out my hand, but she eluded my grasp and glided backward toward the dressing-room, with her beautiful, sorrowful eyes looking straight into mine, as if trying to tell me something, or as if making a mute appeal for aid.

"'What is the matter?' I asked, but she did not answer, and, as she turned her lovely, appealing face from me toward the dark closet, I knew it was nothing mortal—*knew* it was some shade or apparition—something without flesh and blood—for it disappeared before my very eyes like a dissolving mist or wreath of smoke. I then looked in the closet and, indeed, tried the windows and searched the whole house carefully, but saw no more of the strange appearance. Now, the question is, *who* was it? or, Was it an optical illusion or an imaginary spirit?"

"The house is haunted," replied his aunt. "There is no doubt of it. You and your sister have both seen Eulalie's spirit!"

"Pshaw, aunt! What nonsense! Eulalie was always so sweet and smiling. Why should her ghost be always crying? It was the most sorrowful face I ever saw. I can call up no picture of life or of imagination that will correspond with it," he answered

"Well, I can," said Katherine, wiping her eyes. "Eula's dying countenace was like it—its very counterpart. That is why I instantly recognized the one I saw the day we left the house."

"Oh, that accounts for your recognizing it. Association and memory, with the aid of imagination, painted your picture, but not mine. I was away, you know, when she died. You never wrote me about her weeping, or her unwillingness to die; consequently, I could not have recalled a picture I never saw."

"Perhaps there was a hole in one of the shutters and shades, forming a natural *camera obscura*. The figure you both saw may have been some weeping Niobe residing in the house across the way," suggested Mrs. Gaye.

The Lieutenant and his sister laughed. "No," said Katherine, "or the figure would have been inverted like all other sun pictures."

"Very true, Katherine, but we both saw it—on the stairs, too.

What puzzles me the most is the mournful expression. What does it mean? Is she still unhappy? Does she blame us for letting her die? The theory of her dying haunting one's imagination and consciousness is not, *can not,* be true, in my case. The camera idea we have exploded on scientific principles. No living being could have cast her shadow into those rooms except through the keyhole, and, even then, not on the bed. Those rooms were sufficiently light for me to see every object distinctly."

The last time I heard from the Gayes they were living in Europe. Their Philadelphia home was closed and had been advertised for sale, and the question *who was* it is still unanswered.

I have since heard that the Gaye mansion and grounds have been sold, and reconstructed into one large office building and two apartment houses. There is now no use of trying to seek for a secret door or panel, but is it not probable, or, at least, possible, that the weeping ghostess was one of the maids or sempstresses who was familiar with the place and had obtained permission of the caretaker to lodge there, free of rent, or else had a key to a side door and was living there secretly; or, she might have been unknown to the custodian, playing upon the credulity of the dead girl's friends to avoid detection, while she searched and looted Eula's apartments.

"Or, may she not have hidden in some chest or locker in the dark closet?" asks the skeptic.

CHAPTER VIII.

PSYCHOLOGICAL IMPRESSIONS.

We all have, in a greater or less degree, psychological impressions and intuitions—although people of keen perceptive faculties and cultured imaginations are more subject to illuminated thoughts than their opposites. In other words, some organisms are more delicate and susceptible than others.

How often have we awakened with a feeling, or fancy, that "something is going to happen," with a depressed state of mind which we try vainly to shake off, a nameless dread which hangs like a threatening rain cloud over our spirits, but which has explained itself to us after the receipt of a telegram or letter containing bad news, or, hearing of some death or accident, as the "coming event" which had cast such an unaccountable unrest, for a time, over our spirits?

> "And deep misgivings on his spirit fell
> That all with Udolph's household was not well,
> That augers griefs inevitably near,
> Yet, makes them not less startling to the ear."
> —From *Campbell's "Theodorie."*

The above experience is as old as the world of mankind. In the above poem Campbell says that Udolph, soon after the above premonition, arrived in England with the unwelcome tidings of

Julia's approaching death. In another poem, "Lochiel's Warning," the same author says:

> " 'Tis the science of life gives us mystical lore,
> And coming events cast their shadows before."

Said events did transpire. Says the talented Bishop F.: "God does not need to suspend a law of nations to save a good man who may be walking beneath a falling crag. His attention attracted for a moment would keep him from under it at the critical moment. A Colonel, a good class leader, also, at Petersburg, eating his breakfast, sat with his back against a tree. Suddenly he felt constrained to spring down behind the breastworks, and did so. A bullet struck the tree just where he had been sitting. A sharpshooter, in a tree over in the rebel lines, had fixed his eye on him, and God had His eye on the sharpshooter and took His servant out of the way. God is our Father." Is it unnatural to believe that an omnipresent God warned the Colonel of danger?

Rollin says, in his "Ancient History," "Our knowledge of Socrates would be defective if we knew nothing of the genius which, he said, assisted him in the greatest part of his actions. It is not agreed among authors what that genius was. It was commonly called the 'Demon of Socrates,' which signifies something of a divine nature. This genius diverted him from his designs, where prejudicial to him, but never prompted him to undertake any action. He received, also, the same impulse when his friends were going to engage in any unlucky affair which they communicated to him. Now, what does this imply, but a mind, which, by its own lights and a knowledge of mankind, has attained a sort of futurity? In fact, Zenophon understood him to mean that it was the aid of divine wisdom, which speaks in every man by the voice of reason."

I saw the following incident in a Scranton daily dated March 25, 1884: "A gentleman named F. had an unusual impression last night. It was a very windy night, and, thinking that the windows and shutters rattled so loudly that a burglar could enter his house as noisily as he pleased without being heard, he took the precaution of leaving a jet of gas burning in his bed-chamber, and, for the first time in seven years, put a revolver under his pillow. About midnight, on suddenly awakening out of a sound sleep, he saw the figure of a man reflected in the looking-glass opposite his bed.

"If I make a movement he will shoot me," he thought. "I will give a sudden scream and frighten him out of the room." His scream in all probability saved his life. But what made Mr. F. take such precautions on that especial night, of all the windy nights in the year? A man who had been totally deaf for many years, an old friend of mine, whose age was about one hundred years, and while in his usual health fancied that he heard some one calling him. He kept asking, "Did you call me?" or saying, "I hear somebody calling me! I am going to die." The call so worried Mr. S. that he went to his bed declaring, like Christian, that he had "received an order to prepare to go up higher." I can still hear his old, thin, quavering voice saying, "I hear somebody calling for me, I am going to die!" And he did die, in a very few days. "Did he hear anything?" do you ask. Yes. I think the ears of his soul in some way received an intimation of his approaching change of worlds.

One of my neighbors awoke one morning last May with a strong impression that he was going to be killed by the cars. He told his family that he was afraid to go to work. "You do not know how dangerous my business, coupling cars, is," he said. Then his children urged him not to go, and his wife admonished him to be careful. "I will try to be cautious," he answered. "At any rate, this is my last week in the round house yard." A few hours later he was struck by an engine and killed. Why did he dread his work and experience so much fear that particular morning?

One of my friends had a haunting fear of being buried alive. She died a few months ago, the bride of a year. Her death was sudden, but not unexpected to herself. On the day of her funeral her body was so limp and warm that the burial was postponed. On the following Sunday the interment was made, for a change had taken place in the color and temperature of the corpse on Saturday night. She must have been alive on Thursday, and, had they buried her then, her fear would have been realized.

The Hon. "X. Y. Z.," I will call him, a Christian gentleman, who is well known in business circles, for he has filled some of the most important positions in the State of Pennsylvania, says: "I have ever present to my consciousness a guardian angel whom I call my *Financial Monitor*. Before any important business transaction or speculation, where possible failure is involved, and —as it has often proved, actual loss and disappointment might otherwise have resulted—I have always received an intuitive warning. Something has told me not to venture. Whenever I have obeyed my voiceless guardian L have been saved from financial embarrassment and ruinous loss of credit; but the opposite result has followed my disregard of this inward monitor. For instance:

"Last winter, without any previous thought, fear or intimation, I suddenly received the impression that my bank account was short, and immediately said to my wife: 'I fear that something is wrong at the bank. I cannot imagine what it is, for only this morning there were several hundred dollars to my credit, and I have neither given a check nor drawn any money myself to-day.' She laughingly rejoined: 'One of your nervous fancies, again. I would advise you to dismiss it from your mind and go to sleep.'

"But I could not sleep. I ordered an early breakfast, as I wanted to go to town before the bank was opened, but, before I was ready to start, a message was brought requesting my presence at the bank immediately. I looked at my wife with an 'I-told-you-so' expression and started. The cashier received me kindly. 'We sent for you, knowing that you would make it all right; but—the truth is—your account has been overdrawn.' I found that a check which I had given eight months earlier and had, I supposed, been cashed, had not been presented at the bank until the day before. I made it all right, of course, but what, or *who*, my monitor is, is still a puzzling question."

An impression that he was to be killed that day made one of my cousins, the conductor of a train, after leaving home one morning, feel impelled to return and say "good-bye" again to his young bride, to whom he was tenderly attached. He not only acted upon the impulse of the moment, but actually returned the third time and kissed her good-bye before going to his train.

Poor fellow! In less than an hour from their final parting he was brought home a mangled corpse! The sight of her dead husband made his wife a raving maniac for years. Whence came the impression? A young man, after living beyond his income, forged a note on his employer for a large amount, and, on finding that discovery and disgrace, as well as ruin, were inevitable, resolved to commit suicide. He was about to fling himself into the river, when his aged mother, who had been taking a walk in an unusual direction, appeared upon the scene and saved him from death. "I see now," she cried, "why I felt that I must take a walk to the river this morning." But who told her to walk then and to that especial place? Truly, we are of more value in God's eyes "than many sparrows!"

I am indebted to Richmal Mangnall's Universal History and Biography of Distinguished Persons, and Rev. John Mitford's Life of Dean Swift, for the following:

"It is said that the celebrated Dean Swift entertained an apprehension that he should survive his reason. So strong was this presentiment that he left the bulk of his fortune for the erection of a hospital for idiotic and insane people. Dr. Young says that while walking out with Swift and some others near Dublin that he suddenly missed Mr. Dean Swift, who had remained behind the rest of the company. He turned back and found Mr. Swift gazing intently at the top of a lofty elm which was blasted. Upon Young's approach he pointed to it, saying, 'I shall be like that tree, *I shall die first at the top.*'" "Three years before his death," says his biographer, "he experienced that most dreadful of all human calamities, insanity." After some months this great man sank into an idiotic state, which lasted the remainder of his life.

Presentiments of approaching death have been common in all ages.

I picked up an old volume entitled, "The Spiritual Companion," printed in London in 1764, in which was a letter written by a pious English lady to her husband about a century and a half ago, and delivered to him *after her death,* in which she said her mind was filled with apprehensions of her "approaching death." I will give a few extracts from it.

"The sun of prosperity has shone upon me for five years, and I have been blest with one of the best of husbands, which makes the parting stroke most sensibly painful to me. If it were not for the great realities of religion I could not give up the beloved of my heart. All the powers of my soul are at work, when I think what your feelings will be in the trying hour of separation. * * * Nothing now presents itself to me but sorrow, anguish, weeping friends, the gloomy appendages of death and of the opening grave. * * * If you see me in my coffin, rejoice over me and say, 'What was mortal, worms shall destroy, but her soul, arrayed in the robe of the Redeemer's righteousness, lives, to die no more.'" The lady was not suffering from any incurable disease when she wrote the above letter. Her prediction became true.

How am I to account for the sudden impulse which sent the mother of the late Doctor Francis Wayland to her husband's study one day, exclaiming: "Pray for our son, for he is in danger," when, at that very moment, as subsequent reports proved, her son, then a youth, who was absent on a trip up the Hudson River, had fallen overboard, and was in imminent danger of drowning? The Waylands resided on Frankfort street, New

York City, at that time.* How was that mother informed that her son was in danger of drowning? What secret spirit telegraphy was at work between her consciousness and his? In the same paper from which I have taken the above, Mr. Wilder says: "Occurrences like this are not uncommon. John Calvin, the reformer, while sick at Geneva, heard the music and clangor of a battle that was then going on near Paris, between the partisans of the Duke of Guise and the Huguenots." He says of Apillonius: "He was addressing an audience at Ephesus, when the murder of the Emperor Domitian occurred at Rome, and described it, as it occurred, through his power of second sight." These facts, which have been handed down to us through the pages of biography and history, are too well authenticated to be doubted. Had they occurred in these days of telegrams and telephones we might be more skeptical. The same writer says: "Emanuel Swedenborg, in like manner, described a fire in Stockholm, while it was burning, being (himself) at the same time in Gottenburg. Dr. Doddrige's dream may be classed with prophetic visions."

A celebrated writer says: "People of strong imaginations usually find what they are looking for." That means, I suppose, that those who are always looking for supernatural appearances expect to see them and are not disappointed in their expectations. Well, if this is not conceding that there are *ghosts* seen by those who are *looking* for them, it must mean that we can imagine anything when we set ourselves about it.

Another writer, Prof. Austin Phelps, D.D., says that "death is to all minds alike, a dread, appalling prospect, from its first con-

*Copied from A. Wilder's article in *Phrenological Journal,* of Aug., 1872.

ception till life's close. Say what men may of it, all men fear it." He says that "the most devout Christian and the most sensuous skeptic recoil from it, resist it, put it out of sight, struggle to forget it, to the last. It is the one overwhelming terror of every human life."

The only hope we have of a happy hereafter is found in the Bible and the story of Christ's life, death and resurrection; for, because He lived and rose from the grave and ascended into heaven, we shall rise from the dead and live also, if worthy, in the glorious hereafter; and, in Our Father's house of many mansions be reunited with our beloved who have washed their earthly sins away by repentance and holy lives.

Prophetic visions are not confined to the world of fiction. These *Soul Illuminations* are common occurrences in real life.

One of the most intellectual ladies I have ever met said to me: "I believe in soul illuminations. My mind has often received a sudden foreknowledge of subsequent events. Let me tell you a love story. It will illustrate my meaning.

"The first time I ever saw Dr. King I said to myself: 'That man will be my husband!' I did not meet him at that time, only saw him in a crowd, but the conviction that I was to be his future bride had so fastened itself upon my mind that in an instant the thought was an old one—seemed to me a foregone conclusion. 'Yes,' I added aloud, 'I shall marry that man!'

"'The idea!' said a lady friend. 'He is only passing through town, on his way to Boston. You will, in all probability, never see him again.'

"'Oh, yes, I shall,' I answered, confidently. 'He will as surely come back as will another morning.' She laughed incredulously and actually stared at me, as if I had taken leave of my senses. 'But what makes you think so?' she finally found voice to ask. 'I do not *think*—I simply *know* it,' I replied; 'but how, or from what source I obtained this knowledge I am not able to say. An hour ago I did not know of his existence.' A month later Dr. King returned, and, to my great joy, sought an introduction. When he asked me to become his wife I was not at all surprised, but said 'Yes.'"

CHAPTER IX.

HOW HE FOUND HIS IDEAL.

WHILE at Seaview, last summer, I made the acquaintance of Mr. and Mrs. John Warden, the most interesting and charming couple I ever met. We boarded in an ancient, two-story house, whose roof and sides were covered with mossy shingles. There was a large front yard filled with gnarled apple and quince trees and beds of old-fashioned flowers. A row of silver maples divided the garden from the sandy beach. There were a few rustic seats under the maples, where we often sat for hours, watching the restless waves, which came roaring and thundering over the white, pebbly beach, until they broke within a few feet of us on the sand.

It is said that "three are too many," but I did not feel that such was the case while in their society, for we had many delightful conversations together.

I had been an advocate of marrying opposites; but, after noting the almost perfect similarity of temperaments, tastes and talents, as well as the oneness of thought and reciprocity of feeling which existed between them, I felt obliged to change my mind; for a more happily united pair I never expect to find again in this world. They were people of refinement and culture, for both had been blessed with a university education. They not only sketched, painted and sang, but played on several musical instruments and conversed well. Both were fond of rowing, yachting and athletic games, and were engaged in literary pursuits of a high order.

I once remarked to Mr. Warden that I never saw two people so much alike as himself and wife, and he answered:

"That is because I married my *ideal*. I will tell you how I found her; and if you do not agree with me that 'marriages are made in heaven,' I shall be greatly mistaken. I had reached the age of thirty years without falling in love with any one except an imaginary woman. My home, for years, had been in New York City—my profession that of a journalist. I was a partner in the proprietorship of a certain live periodical, and had, just before the commencement of my story, been elected junior editor. One evening I received a call from the head of the firm, and, after a lengthy consultation and he was about to leave, he remarked: 'It strikes me that you are living in single wretchedness too long. You are now abundantly able to support a wife, and, as you are a rising young man, can certainly have no difficulty in finding a lady to your taste in your circle of acquaintances. My advice is, take a partner for life. Good night.' 'Thank you,' I soliloquized, 'for your unasked council, but I shall never marry unless I can find my *ideal*,' and, taking up my hat, I started for the Academy. A celebrated lecturer was already on the platform. I took my seat and looked toward the speaker, when the magnetic power of a pair of eyes at my left caused me to turn quickly around, and there I beheld, for the first time, in physical presence, a *fac-simile* of the ideal face which had haunted my mental vision for three years, rendering me indifferent to all the charms of my lady friends.

"Yes, as true as you live, I had seen those very dark, soul-lit eyes, those firmly cut, crimson lips, that pure, broad, intellectual forehead shaded with clustering curls. That dark, sparkling, patrician face with its rich coloring, had often appeared to me in my sleeping and waking dreams; had smiled at me from amid flitting ember pictures, time and time again, until I had grown so familiar with it that when its owner willed that I should look around I simply recognized it as the reality of my manhood's ideal.

"As our eyes met, a crimson flush, accompanied by an expression of soul recognition, flashed over her countenance, and she turned toward the lecturer, but again and again I could feel, without looking at her, that her eyes were burning upon my face.

"The lecture came to a close, and I lost sight of my *'Blumine'* in the crowd, but as I rode homeward I knew that somewhere, some time, I should meet her again—that her future life would be blended with mine. Occasionally a restless longing for her tangible presence took possession of my soul, but my time was so entirely occupied that I had very little leisure for idle day dreams.

"I was boarding at the A— House that year, and one evening, several months later, I met a lady in the corridor, who, although closely veiled, reminded me of my lovely dream-wife. That night I dreamed that the hotel was on fire, that my ideal was being burned alive in a certain room—No. 48—on the second floor. I was suddenly awakened by the cry of 'Fire!' sounding through the house. I sprang out of bed and dressed myself, then I hastened to the left wing of the second story, instead of following the terrified crowd downstairs. The impression of my dream was still so strong upon me that all thoughts of self-preservation or personal fear were merged into solicitude for the safety of the unknown lady. I feared that the fire had broken out in that quarter, for the hall was filled with smoke. I finally reached No. 48 and found, to my horror, that the door was locked! As the house was heated by a furnace, I knew the smoke must have crept up through the flues and filled her room. I threw myself against the door with almost superhuman strength, but it would not yield to my frantic efforts.

"'This is terrible! She will be burned alive!' I cried. I then crept through the transom, and found the lady of my dream lying half-way across the room, unconscious from the poisonous gases. The flames were already creeping into the apartment. With a hasty spring, I unlocked the door and carried her out into the corridor, which was already on fire. I remember that we were being carried through the smoke and flames into the outer air in the arms of strong men, just as the roof and second floor fell in, sending a shower of crimson sparks around. Then a blank followed and for weeks I lay very near death's door. Recovery came at last, with only a few deep, hideous scars on my breast and arms to remind me of that strange adventure.

"I was told that I had received my injuries while rescuing a transient boarder—name unknown—for the hotel register was burned.

"Some months after this I was sent to Germany as special correspondent for our paper. As I was still somewhat weak, I was glad of the ocean voyage and change of air and scene. In the autumn I concluded to make a trip through Switzerland.

"At times, however, I felt during that journey that my dream-wife was not far off, as if I were walking in her very footsteps, breathing the very air she breathed. One glorious afternoon in autumn, while I was sitting in a charming valley sketching Mont Blanc, an uncontrollable longing to behold my ideal once more took posession of my thoughts. It seemed as if she were somewhere in sight, thinking of me—looking at me. My love for her had grown stronger with each passing day. I had never, since I first saw her, forgotten to pray for her welfare. I felt that I was working for her, improving myself for her sake. I believed she was a pure, unselfish, loving, refined woman; that she was beautiful in her heart and soul, as well as in mind and person.

"Well, as I was sketching, my thoughts took visible form, and before I was aware of the change Mont Blanc melted away into misty clouds, and in its place the face of my unknown smiled up at me from my temporary easel. I was so wholly absorbed in my occupation that I did not notice the approach of a party of American tourists until an old college friend, Jim Dalton, slapped me on the shoulder, exclaiming:

"'John Warden, as I live, and painting your likeness, cousin Belle!' as he grasped my hand, adding: 'I have been following you around from place to place for the past month, and was always a day or two too late to see you. Allow me to present my cousin, Isabel Holmes, and Uncle Timothy, her father. You have heard me speak of him, often.' I arose and bowed to the lady, and was not surprised to see the original of the pictured face on my canvas. She had caught a glimpse of my picture, and, as our eyes met, a blush suffused her cheeks. We shook hands and the magnetism of her hand thrilled every nerve with a nameless joy, and when she lifted her glorious eyes to mine I felt that we loved each other with a deathless affection—that I had *found the other half of my being*.

"'A striking coincidence,' said Jim, as he opened her portfolio and showed me a sketch of myself that she had made from memory that very day.

"I asked where she had seen me.

"'At a lecture in New York and at the A— House the night of the fire. I saw you as I passed through the lower hall on my way to my room.' She subsequently told me that she had dreamed of seeing me the night before she saw me at the Academy, and recognized me as the hero of her vision. 'I had the same clairvoyant perception of your presence at the A— House the night of the fire. Were you really there? And this afternoon I have felt for the third time in my life the certainty of your presence, as if your thoughts pervaded the atmosphere around me.'

"We finished our tour together. Belle returned to her home on the Hudson, to prepare for the wedding, and I went to my old quarters in New York. Of course, I was very happy, for she had promised to become my wife in the early spring.

"It often happened that whenever I was writing to her she was penning a letter to me at the same time. No matter how unexpectedly I visited her, she would say:

"'Something has told me all day that I should see you to-night, John.'

"We seemed to influence each other's minds and movements independently of distance or time; and, incredible as it may seem, could almost read each other's thoughts.

"One February morning as I was seated in Trinity Church, listening to an impressive discourse, I suddenly seemed to see her standing before me. She wore a long, flowing robe of white, and her abundant black hair, which you know ripples and waves to its very roots, fell over her shoulders like a veil. Her face wore the most agonized expression, and her arms were extended toward me pleadingly. The vision vanished in a moment, but, for the first time, I found that I could not listen to the clergyman intelligently. Before the services were over I left the church, hastened to the nearest telegraph office and sent the following message: 'Belle, is anything the matter?' In reply came this telegram: 'Yes, father is dying! Come to me.' I went, and found that Mr. Holmes had been seized with a paralytic stroke while getting ready for church.

"Belle met me at the door, clad in the identical white robe I had seen in my vision. As I passed my hand caressingly over her floating hair, she explained:

"'I have not been able to leave father for a minute since he was taken ill. You must pardon my *dishabille*. Strange as it may seem, when father fell from his chair I though he was dead, and instantly felt such a strong desire for your presence that my thoughts must have acted upon yours, my will influenced your own. I can account for your solicitude in no other way. I should have wired you sooner—pardon me, John.'

"Her father died that night, without recovering consciousness, and after he was laid to rest in the quiet cemetery beside his wife, who had gone to Heaven years before, we had a quiet wedding; for Belle was all alone and needed my protection. We rented her cottage on the Hudson and went to the metropolis to reside."

Mrs. Warden now joined us. She looked so fresh and joyous, and withal so beautiful in her simple, white muslin, with scarlet fuchsias in her midnight hair, that I did not wonder at her husband's lover-like admiration.

You will agree with me that we have all more or less experienced psychological impressions, also, that people of cultured imaginations have, or have had, their *ideals?*

CHAPTER X.

THAT SHADOW IN THE PARK.

READER, have you ever seen a ghost? I have. It was a veritable wraith, nothing material about it. The place was in the village of Honesdale, Pa., a town prettily laid out and shaded with maples. The scene, a large park filled with shade trees; a fountain in the centre, and near it a monument dedicated to the soldiers who fell in the Civil War. Surrounding this lovely park are fine residences and public buildings. The hour was 6 o'clock in the winter evening. The street lamps were not yet lighted. The court house across the square was ablaze with light, for court was still in session.

I said to myself as I noted the gathering gloom in that section of the town after leaving the business part of the village: "The people are probably at dinner, and their dining-rooms are in the rear of their parlors, which are not lighted. But how quiet and strangely deserted this street is! I should not like to meet any one here."

I quickened my steps, then stopped with a nameless fear. Do you ask what I saw? A tall man in a soldier's garb, with a bayonet in his hand. He was walking in mid-air only a few feet from me, on my left. His feet were as high as the second story windows. I held my breath as I gazed at the spectre. "Why does it walk in mid-air?" The wild beating of my heart and soft splashing of the fountain alone broke the silence. I tried to fling off the incubus, but could not, as I studied the weird figure. It was so transparent that I could see through it. Again I moved on, but without taking my eyes from it, and, lo! my shadowy attendant moved on, too. I paused in my walk—my soldier friend did the same. I retraced my steps a few feet—so did my escort. Then I knew that it was only the shadow of the bronze figure which surmounted the soldiers' monument in the park. The light from the court house windows behind the monument had, of course, thrown this shadow across the square, but it was the most perfect shade I ever saw.

As far as I can ascertain, none of my acquaintances ever saw this ghost of the park as it appeared to my vision that evening, nor have I seen it since, either, although I have passed the same spot many times, both before and after lamps were lighted.

By a proper investigation ninety-nine out of every one hundred so-called hobgoblins which the ages have seen would have been found to be as harmless as my shadowy friend in the park.

That our shadows always follow or precede us, is true. They

never leave us. Where is the individual who has not been frightened by his or her shadow? I have, often. Nothing disconcerts me more, or makes the cold chills creep over me sooner, than to see my silent shadow flitting up or downstairs before me in the twilight. I again confess that I do not like shadows. Once, in going to my room in a New York hotel at night, I was startled at seeing the figure of a woman flitting along the long, dimly lighted corridor before me, but I could not hear her footsteps. I stopped and listened. The woman stopped, too. I went on, and she went on, too. The reader will readily guess the rest.

CHAPTER XI.

A YOUNG WIFE'S TRIAL.

"Who did sin, this man or his parents?"

"LOVE is a strange god, but I suppose he 'must go where he is sent," whispered Mrs. Lake to her right-hand neighbor, as they waited in the old ivy-covered church on College Green, on Helen Ward's wedding morning.

"True, madam. 'There is no accounting for tastes,'" was the smiling rejoinder of Mrs. Greene.

"No; but who would have thought a scientist like Prof. Ward would have allowed his young and charming daughter to become the wife of a *deformed* man, no matter how wealthy or talented the gentleman is, or how high his family is in the social scale? They say it is a case of long standing, too; that young Earle fell in love with Miss Helen when he first came to Yale College."

"Perhaps she marries him out of pity?"

"It is possible. Mrs. Ward says that her daughter hesitated a good while before giving him a favorable answer."

"Yet Helen must be strongly attached to him, for she has refused several of the best marrying men in New Haven. I presume the young lady's judgment told her that his deformity was probably hereditary, and might some time in the future reproduce itself. My husband says, 'Deformity, as well as consumption, scrofula or insanity, may have been inherited.'"

"Still, it may make no difference in this case. Although he has a withered hand and foot, and cannot walk without the aid of a cane, the defect is scarcely perceptible to the eye."

"Poor girl! his enviable position and splendid establishment will not repay the sacrifice, I fear. They go to Italy on their wedding tour, I am told."

"Yes. Her *trousseau* is elegant, and her presents are superb and costly. You must see Mr. Earle's gift to the bride—diamonds worth a small fortune. But here they come. How beautiful she is!" added the first speaker, as the wedding party took their places at the altar.

"*Mais,* how white she is growing! She will faint before the ceremony is over," said Mrs. Greene.

The bride did not faint, however, but she looked more like a lovely frozen corpse than her own blooming self, at the altar, and no wonder, for the touch of his cold, flaccid hand sent an icy chill through heart and brain, and awakened again that nameless fear which had made her hesitate so long before accepting William Earle for "better or for worse."

They sailed across the Atlantic, then along the blue Mediterranean, visited the most noted cities and countries of Europe, and, after a year abroad, returned to their palace summer home in the Elm City. Yet amid the glorious scenery of the Old World, the memory of that shivering dread at the altar, of that undefined, shadowy fear, came constantly between the young wife and her keenest enjoyments.

Her husband, who was fondly attached to her, anticipated her every known wish, and did all in his power to make her home-life enjoyable. He surrounded her with treasures of art, and made her home almost as charming as the fabled palace of Aladdin. Yet, although she never complained, he saw a shadow in her eyes, felt that some hidden trouble had changed her laughing, piquant face into one of gentle sadness, in that brief year of wedded life.

"What ails her?" he had asked himself a thousand times, but, man-like, his intuitions were not keen enough to unravel the secret, and his wife brooded over it continually, thus:

"Shall I never be able to bear his caresses without a shudder? Must the sword of Damocles always hang over my defenseless head? Shall I ever dare tell my husband, my best friend, of this dread which is almost undermining my reason? Will he hate me if I tell him, I wonder?"

In the sweet June weather Mrs. Earle lay in her darkened chamber, white and deathlike, oblivious to the loveliness without, or the anxiety which reigned in their home on her account. The fearful struggle between life and death was ended at last, and her husband bent tenderly over her pillow and whispered, as he softly kissed her white lips:

"Oh, Helen, God has been good to us! He has given you back

to me, and added another gift, a son." His words aroused her from the deathly stupor into which she had fallen. The dizziness was all gone in an instant. The purple hue of death receded from her faded lips and cheeks.

"Yes—I remember now. Go bring my baby," she said; "quick! I have named him already. Let me see my wee Willie—I cannot wait. William"—she gasped. He gently took her quivering hands within his own and said, in a hesitating manner:

"Presently, my Helen—only—the doctor says you must sleep first—that you should not excite yourself to-day."

"What! *Sleep* before I have seen my baby? No mother is ever too ill to see her first child." Then, with pretty willfulness, she turned to her nurse, who had approached the bed:

"Mrs. Beebe, bring him to me! I shall die if you keep me in suspense any longer!" The feverish glitter in her eyes warned them not to thwart her wishes. Baby, enveloped in soft folds of flannel and muslin, was laid upon her bosom. Oh, the nameless bliss which that precious burden awakened in her heart for a moment! Then, like a last night's dream, her old terror returned. She tried to stifle the thought, as she passionately kissed that tiny, quiet face, but the new-born mother love would not be satisfied. How eagerly she scanned the pink arms and tiny hands, and peered at his silken eyelids or the rings of soft hair over his broad forehead.

"I wonder if he can see? Nurse, open that blind a moment, and let the light fall on his face." As the sunbeams streamed across the bed the infant opened his round, blue eyes.

"Yes, he can see; but I wonder if he can hear?" Just then the little cuckoo clock on the mantel sang out the noon hour, making baby cry out like a startled bird. "Yes, the darling can hear—he is not dumb, either. Now—I must see his pretty feet." Her husband and nurse exchanged glances and tried to take the babe from her trembling hands, but she held him closer, and, panting for breath, sobbed hysterically:

"I will—I *must* see if his limbs and feet are perfect!" Then she drew back his wrappings and before they could prevent it, saw with horrible distinctness that her boy would be a *helpless cripple for life.* His lower extremities were terribly deformed—were twisted, shapeless stumps, *without feet.* Her husband's infirmity *had been transmitted to the child* in a more dreadful form. The mother's head fell back on her pillow, as she moaned brokenly:

"Oh, husband! The thing I most dreaded has come upon me! I have loved the beautiful all my life, and hated deformity and monstrosity. Take this *thing* from my sight—let me never look upon it again! I expected this—the thought has haunted me for months. If prayers, or tears, or *love* could have availed, this blow would not have fallen. Surely, God has been unkind to me! My life is a failure—a cruel nightmare!" She paused from mere exhaustion. Her husband endeavored to soothe her with tender caresses. She motioned him away, with a frown, and raved: "Take your hated hand from my head. It scorches my very brain! Let it never touch me again! As Heaven is my witness, I will never bear you another *cripple,* William Earle!" she deliriously cried, then relapsed into a deadly syncope.

The June days had drifted into July before Helen Earle awoke to consciousness and asked for her child.

"It is gone," said her mother, "but is better off than it could have been with us, dear. So do not fret about it, but for the sake of us who love you try to get well."

"Yes, mother, you are right. Wee Willie will not be *lame* in Heaven," she calmly answered.

"That he will not, my daughter. Now drink this, and think of your boy as—"

"With the angels," Mrs. Earle added.

The days came and went, but alas! returning health brought no joy to the young mother. If she could have felt that her baby was dead, that he was really at rest under the daisies, it would have been a relief to her; but something told her continually that he was still a living reproof to her for disregarding the laws of nature and common sense. In spite of reason, she had a vivid impression that he was not only alive, but was near her night and day. Another thing began to worry her, as the summer days grew shorter. Her once devoted husband had scarcely spoken to her alone, since her convalescence. He would accompany the physician or her friends to her boudoir, or ask Nurse Beebe at the door how his wife was, or send her hot-house flowers or choice fruits every morning; bought new books or magazines for her daily; was uniformly polite and kind, yet she knew that he purposely avoided an interview with her. She was certain that her bitter words on that day had killed his love and respect for her.

At first, so stupified had her brain become during her long illness that she regarded his apparent coldness with indifference; but, as September drew near, she felt a strong desire for reconciliation. The conviction that she had been the most to blame, that by brooding over a fancied misfortune she had been instrumental in bringing it about, finally forced itself upon her mind. She thought tearfully: "My own miserable nervousness and pride have been the cause of all our unhappiness. My husband *must* pardon my blind folly! I can bear his coldness no longer." Then, rushing into the library, she fell upon her knees beside his chair and begged his forgiveness. He raised her up and took her in his arms. Told her that his regards for her had not changed; that he had not inflicted his presence upon her, supposing she wished to be left alone, and took the blame of her sickness upon himself, poor fellow, for marrying. Said he:

"Mrs. Ellis was right when she wrote: 'All deformed, diseased, little and ugly people should never marry.' I do not quote it correctly, perhaps, but the writer was wiser than myself."

Then his wife told him how hungry she was for a glimpse of her baby's grave: "Somehow, he is not dead to me. I have such a singular mental perception of his presence constantly. Strange as it may seem to you, I nightly rock my imaginary baby to sleep in my arms. I must see his grave."

"I think, Helen, that you had better defer your visit to the cemetery until next spring," he answered.

"But I really cannot wait. It does not seem to me that he is *there*. I dream of him every night. Last evening I saw him in a little carriage stretching out his arms toward me. I keep a bright light in my rooms all night, for Baby's face haunts me in the dark. How can you account for these strangely vivid hallucinations?"

He gave her an evasive answer, then told her to get ready for a drive. They drove out on the West Haven road, several miles into the country. The September day was beautiful. Its robe of crimson, orange and scarlet tints and rich browns, its green and amber-colored ferns, the grasses and reddening creeping vines with the sun's golden lances slanting obliquely through all this variegated foliage; the intense blue of the sky, awakened again Helen's artistic love for color and stirred anew the passionate depths of her woman's heart. She gathered a great bunch of golden-rod by the roadside.

"We have each other to live for still," said her husband, noting the happy expression of her countenance for the first time since her illness.

"Yes, William, while I have *you*, I will try to be contented and thankful," she replied, as they stopped in front of a small, white cottage, which was nearly covered with a scarlet Virginia creeper, and surrounded by locust and ailanthus trees. In the shady front yard, a young nursery maid was wheeling a perambulator in which was an infant in a white cloak and hood, and was about three months old. He smiled and waved his tiny hands when the Earles halted at the gate.

"If our boy had lived he would have been like that child," said Mr. Earle. His wife looked at the infant a moment, then sprang out of the carriage, exclaiming:

"This is the very baby I have dreamed about so often, William! Is it our lost Wee Willie? Were my instincts true, after all?"

When Mr. Earle reached the happy mother, she was crying for joy, and showering kisses upon the little one's poor dwarfed limbs and "clump" feet.

Of course, they took their baby boy home with them, and her husband explained:

"I intended to undeceive you, Helen, as soon as you were able to see him, my dear."

Peace like the fabled Hestia, again presided over their hearthstone. They both learned to love Willie very dearly; but at the age of three years, a pitying Jesus called the little boy home. His mother wrote to a friend soon after his death: "We have another son, Wee Willie's *fac-simile*—only his form and face, hands and limbs are as perfect as Raphael's picture of the infant Jesus. It almost seems to us that our lost one's soul has taken possession of this new and lovely body. I tried hard, after I regained my health, to keep my mind at rest on this one subject, believing that it was my own nervous dread that caused my first-born's malformation. I would like to lift a warning voice to all women who are addicted to borrowing trouble and meeting it half-way. Fancied trials often become realities. I believe that a calm reliance upon our Heavenly Father's care will prevent such calamities under nearly all circumstances."

Helen Earle has had her lesson. She undoubtedly brought her sorrow upon herself by allowing her mind to dwell so persistently upon her husband's deformity. If she had loved him better, or placed more confidence in a protecting Providence, it is probable that the affliction which nearly wrecked her happiness would have been averted. By fretting over and fostering any pre-natal delusion or cause of mental disturbance, great harm may be done to others, while untold sorrow and mortification must be the portion of the one who causes this irremediable injury. On the other hand, as in Mrs. Earle's latter experience, the happiest results follow an unwavering determination to allow no unpleasant thoughts or fears to agitate the mind.

It is a pity that this theory will not hold true in all cases of hereditary disease, and, especially those infirmities which result from the use of ardent spirits. It is a great privilege *to build a house for an immortal soul,* and it must be a crime equal to deicide to destroy one of these "temples of the living God!" because subsequent repentance or the plea of ignorance can never rebuild this glorious temple.

But how did she get the vivid impression that her child was alive and near her?

CHAPTER XII.

TONGUELESS VOICES.

My great-grandfather's home was in New Jersey, six miles from the shore. His only brother, John Hoell, was a sea captain, and owned a sailing vessel. One night, when Captain Hoell's ship was due, and during the progress of one of the fiercest equinoxial gales which ever raged along the stormy New Jersey coast, my great-grandfather was so uneasy about his brother that he walked the house for hours in the greatest anxiety. He was finally compelled by exhaustion to lie down and rest, but he always declared that no sooner had he sought his pillow than a voice cried out: "Your brother John and six of his men are drowned." My great-grandfather sprang out of bed and soon rode to the shore, where he found to his sorrow that his brother's ship had been wrecked upon the rocks. The dead bodies of the captain and six of his crew were left upon the sands by the incoming tide soon after daybreak. (*An actual occurrence*—proven by family records.) Do you ask, who communicated the tidings of that shipwreck to the captain's brother? I cannot tell, neither could he; for he was alone at the time—and the only one who was awake in the house.

Had a human voice called to him from without, he could not have heard it above the roar of the thunder, wind and rain.

"Passavant says, "Two persons at a distance can compel thoughts and dreams. Two people think the same thoughts simultaneously. Why do we think of another when he is coming to visit us? Are there beings devoid of a visible body who are cognizant of our thoughts?" Have we guardian angels? Why not? "In heaven their spirits do always behold the face of the Father," said Christ. A good deal is said and written about brain waves, wave impressions, the twilight of psychological science, psychical phenomena, unconscious cerebration, uncontrollable impulse, molecular activity, spontaneous mental action, perception and intuition, ratiocination, transcendentalism, spectral visitants, spiritual clairvoyance, or soul-illumination; but what do we *know* about them, after all? Nothing, to a certainty; I must acknowledge.

Yet it is possible that Captain Hoell, while drowning, sent a brain wave to his brother, or spirit telegram, compelling the ears of his soul to listen and the eyes of his soul to see. Their thoughts were bent intently, agonizingly, upon each other, and, according to Passavant, compelled my great-grandfather to listen to the tongueless voice of a vivid IMPRESSION. Or, *was it a* DREAM?

My readers will remember a story which went the rounds of the newspapers a few years ago, entitled "The Engineer's Story," I presume. How, when at midnight, while running an express train over one of the highest and most dangerous pieces of trestle-work which spans the Catawissa hills, he distinctly heard a voice say, "Stop," and, although going at the rate of sixty miles per hour, he immediately whistled, "Down brakes!" When the train came to a dead stop the brakeman nearest and fireman both asked why he had whistled down brakes. "Why," he exclaimed, "did you not tell me to stop?" "No," was the reply, "there is nothing wrong on the track." Then the conductor came up and the engineer told him that he had heard a voice say, "Stop!" and had obeyed it. "It was no human voice," said his companions. "You imagined it," said the conductor. "No, I heard that word *'Stop!'* as plainly as I hear you speak," was the answer, and, seizing a lantern, he ran a few yards ahead, and found a *broken rail* and a portion of the trestle-work missing. But for this timely warning the express would, in all probability, have been precipitated into the yawning chasm below, and a hundred souls hurried into eternity without a moment's preparation. What was the voice, or, rather, *whose* voice was it? There could have been no one around on that trestle at that hour of the night, or, even if there had been, the engineer could not have heard it at the rate in which his train was thundering along, and they were miles from any human habitation. Again, who gave the warning? Did the engineer hear anything, or was it simply another searchlight impression? Or, was it the voice of God speaking to his soul? Or, could an angel have spoken to him? "It is possible," you will answer. "God once sent His angel's voice through the mouth of a dumb beast to warn Balaam, and may not such things happen now, as well as in old Bible days?"

But why do not all engineers and conductors and brakemen have such warnings before railway accidents? Alas! why not?

Before the death of a sister I saw a face bending over me while I was lying awake. It was like one of Raffael's pictured angels, but more beautiful.

A lady told me that she always had a warning before a death in her family, either by a dream or seeing some dead face before her. But the face I saw was smiling as it faded away.

"Did you ever have an impression that something dreadful was going to happen?" I asked, "without seeing anything unusual?"

"Oh, yes. I was in church a short time before my eldest son's death. A number of young men were in the pew ahead of me. Suddenly it seemed to me that something said in my ear: 'One of these young men is going to be instantly killed.' I looked around, but no one seemed to have heard it; but the fear that some bereavement was at hand rendered it impossible for me to listen to the sermon. Indeed, it seemed to me that the coming trouble had already happened. The thought was old in an instant after it had entered my mind. On reaching home, I mentioned my still vivid impression to my son. 'Why, mother,' he replied, 'I was just before you in that pew. Of course, if a voice had spoken, or any one had whispered to you, I should have heard. It is all a delusion. You are cultivating imagination to the exclusion of your better judgment.' I did not know that David was there, and told him so. A short time after that he was killed by the explosion of a boiler in a stationary engine—blown sixty feet away from the place of the disaster and picked up a mangled corpse."

Speaking of mysterious noises, or *tongueless voices,* I had a strange experience, or, rather, an unaccountable fright a few nights before the death of a near relative. I was the only one in the house who was awake at the time—2 o'clock in the morning—for the sick man and his wife were both asleep and there was no one else in the house. The room was very still—only the labored breathing of the invalid was heard, except the ticking of the old-fashioned, tall clock in an adjoining room, when suddenly I was startled by a frightful crash, as if some one had thrown a bomb through the roof or sent a rock or iron ball crashing through the side of the farmhouse. The sick man started and awoke. I sprang up and went to him, for, as usual upon awakening, a paroxysm of coughing had seized him; but, as soon as he was quiet, I awoke his wife and told her what I had just heard. She said: "You must have been asleep and dreaming." "No," I insisted, "I was just lifting this cup of coffee to drink, and, see, I have spilled it all over the table." We went out and examined the house—but there was neither rock, nor board, nor ball to be seen, nor a track in the unbroken snow on that side of the dwelling. My friend died soon afterward. We have never been able to account for the terrible crash which frightened me that night, but I have often wondered what caused it and what it really meant, yet have arrived at no satisfactory answer.

Mrs. Bland, another intimate friend, and her late husband, both members of the Episcopalian Church, had a similar experience. They were educated people and were warmly attached to each other; indeed, I may here say, were the most affectionate couple I ever knew. Mr. Bland was in his usual health, however, when the premonition came. He was startled early on the Sabbath morning before his death by a loud rapping on his front door.

It was light enough to see, and he rushed to his chamber window and looked out to ascertain who might be at his door; but not a soul was to be seen there or on the street. The same sound was repeated again, three times. It sounded all through the house. His wife heard it and went downstairs, but could see nothing. The next day Mr. Bland was taken sick. He died three days afterward. Truth. I am not making fancy pictures. An aunt of mine told me a similar experience. A short time before her eldest son's death her husband heard a crash as if some one had smashed the kitchen range all to pieces with a sledge hammer. He went to the kitchen immediately, but everything was quiet and in order. Yet the sound had been there he always said. A few days later my aunt, when alone in the house, heard a sound under her feet like a terrific explosion. "It sounded as if rocks and timber and iron were all falling around me," she said, "but I could never find any cause for it, as there was nothing out of place in or under the house when I had summoned up courage enough to make an examination of the premises five minutes later." Her eldest son, a young man, was killed in a railroad collision and was found under an engine. His body was brought to his home an unrecognizable mass of mangled flesh and broken bones.

But, if the above-named facts *were* warnings, what good did they do, after all?

In concluding this chapter, let me say, let no one disregard a startling, vivid impression.

Educate the ears of the soul, and listen well to these invisible messengers which speak to you through visions and dreams and impressions.

CHAPTER XIII.

THE WEIRD MUSICIAN.

TEN years ago, while visiting friends in Thistledown, Pa., I was told the following story, and will here relate it, word for word, as it was given, as far as memory will permit:

"Thistledown has just had a sensation," said my hostess, Mrs. Doree, "a veritable ghost story. Shall I tell you about it?"

"Certainly, but I warn you not to impose too much upon my credulity, for I am not very superstitious."

"Oh, I know you are a sad skeptic in such matters. However, this is a true story, an actual occurrence. Did you notice the occupants of the pew directly in front of us this morning at church?"

"Yes. A gentleman, a sweet little girl with a young woman who looked like a nurserymaid. The man wore a light tweed suit, has tawny hair and mustache and the most cynical face I ever saw."

"The same. His name is Cornelius Butterfield. He is a native of London, England, and the little girl is his only child. Pansy, he calls her. He came here five years ago, and entered into partnership with McLeod & Co. His wife, report said, was the daughter of an English nobleman. She was a fair, blue-eyed, delicate-looking lady. Her age was about twenty years. She was highly educated, an accomplished musician, and the most romantic, sensitive being I ever knew. Her maid accompanied her to this country, but after a few weeks returned to England.

"The Butterfields moved into a new, uncomfortable-looking house uptown, where the young wife, who had never dressed herself alone or arranged her gold-colored hair without the aid of her maid, was obliged to do her housework and sewing. Of course, this was very distasteful to one who had been tenderly reared in a luxurious London home. The lady could not help being homesick and unhappy. It is said that she made many mistakes in the culinary department—that her husband was harsh and cruelly impatient with his young, inexperienced wife. Poor thing! He even denied her many of the necessaries as well as all of the luxuries of life, I was told. It seems that it was an elopement. Mrs. Butterfield had a highly cultivated voice. She could play on the piano with taste and expression, but her husband refused to get her an instrument. She would plead with him for hours for a piano, with tears in her eyes, and declare that she should be less homesick if she could amuse herself with music when her work was done; but he did not wish to gratify her in this respect. It is said that her family across the ocean sent frequent sums of money to her. If they did, he must have kept the money, for the piano did not come to cheer her.

"It is reported that he used to beat her, but I am not sure that this was true, although I have heard him scold her for boiling the coffee too much or too little, and then reproach her for crying.

"When I found that she could play so finely, I invited her to come here whenever she had time to practice. She was very thankful, I can assure you; and would come in and sing for hours at a time. I must say again, that I still think Alice Butterfield's touch and voice were both the finest and sweetest I have ever heard. Her selections were new to most of us. Indeed no one in Thistledown could play any of her pieces; for her music was of a higher class than ours, I wish you could have heard her."

"How did it please her husband to have her practice here?" I asked. "Not very well. He told me that she was crazy to sing in public and he wanted to discourage her. That 'she had been trained for the opera.' But, how homesick and *distract* she was before her baby was born! Her playing only seemed to revive old memories and associations; for her cheeks were usually wet with tears when she rose from my piano;—yet one could not question her.

"I did not see her alive after her little girl was born, although I called frequently. The doctor or her husband was always on guard, and would say: 'She is raving with fever, you cannot see her to-day;' or, 'she is sleeping, and ought not to be disturbed.' One day when I went to the foot of the chamber stairs to inquire about her, she heard me, and cried out: 'Let Mrs. Doree come up! I tell you I must and *will* see her!' But the doctor came hurrying downstairs, and told me that his 'patient did not know what she was saying;' that my 'presence might excite her too much.' That, 'her very life depended on her being kept quiet.'

"I went away fearing, I knew not what. She died that night; and when I again called, she was in her coffin. Her husband was present. 'He has never left her since the beginning of her sickness,' the nurse said, 'not even for his meals. He only wanted me to take care of the baby and bring things upstairs when they were needed,' she added, 'He was the real nurse, and the doctor was always in the house. He ordered me to keep her baby out of the sick-room, and people out of the house, as his wife could not be disturbed by visitors. So nobody went into her room except himself and the doctor, but I could hear the poor lady raving and crying all day long for a piano, or money to go home to London, to her mother.'

"Mr. Butterfield and the physician prepared the dead woman for the grave. She was dressed in her beautiful wedding gown, white satin and real lace. A Queen Elizabeth *ruche* was placed high about her neck, and her breast and throat were covered with white roses, for her corsage was cut low. Her face seemed to rise out of a thick mass of white flowers and lace. They buried her very quickly, I think—the second morning after she died. The funeral was private, only a few being present, except the doctor and clergyman. We wondered why the corpse was so profusely decorated with flowers, as she was not a bride. Her dead face was beautiful. It seemed to glorify that poorly furnished apartment, yet Mr. Butterfield, I remember, did not once raise his head from his hands or take one farewell look at his dead wife. After a short prayer they placed the white casket in a hearse and drove directly to the cemetery.

"Mr. Butterfield's apparently undue haste in burying his wife, as well as the privacy attending both her sickness and funeral obsequies, caused no little stir in Thistledown. There was talk of unfair play on the part of her husband and the physician, and a coroner's inquest was spoken of. Then the story leaked out that in her delirium Alice Butterfield had attempted suicide by cutting her throat so badly as subsequently to cause her death. That Dr. Webb had hoped to save his patient until the very last, he said, 'by keeping her quiet, and not allowing any one to see or talk to her until the wound had healed. That is why I excluded everybody except her husband and nurse from the room. But she died from her own hand.'

"Mr. Butterfield's apparent penuriousness ceased soon after his wife's death. He rented a larger house uptown, furnished it handsomely and purchased a grand Steinway piano. He employed a cook and nurserymaid, then sent for his sister to come and preside over his establishment. She came.

"Miss Butterfield was no longer young, but she talked and dressed like a woman accustomed to good society. She played accompaniments for church music and songs, but lacked Alice's nice touch for the piano and classical knowledge of instrumental music, as well as her innate delicacy and fine culture. Still, we rather liked her and tried to make the English lady feel at home with us, although her reserved manner repelled our well-meant overtures of friendship."

About a fortnight after Elizabeth Butterfield's arrival both she and her brother were startled in the dead of the night by hearing some one playing on the new piano. The style of the nocturnal visitor was not only brilliant, but was unmistakably like that of the late Mrs. Alice Butterfield. Instrumental music of a high order, portions of celebrated operas, nocturnes and classical compositions, rarely heard in an inland town like Thistledown. The sweet notes trembled all through the house, thrillingly clear and wonderfully pure, closing with Mendelssohn's wedding march.

Brother and sister and maids rushed downstairs, and stared at each other in alarm when they met at the door of the drawing-room.

"'I thought it was you, Elizabeth,' said Mr. Butterfield.

"'And I thought it was you, Cornelius, but wondered how you had learned to play so well since you left England. But how did the player get in? I have the key in my pocket, upstairs.'

"Her brother tried the door and found it locked, as his sister had said. 'It is very strange,' he whispered, in an awe-struck manner, then to his sister: 'Run and get the key. We will solve this mystery at once.'

"When they opened the door they found that the fine-toned instrument was being played by invisible fingers, for the music still continued, although the music stool was unoccupied and they were the only visible occupants of the room. They listened in alarm—looked at each other with terror-stricken faces until the music ceased. Then Mr. Butterfield asked:

"'Can you play any of those pieces?'

"'No, Cornelius. I never learned any difficult music; you know I only play simple chords and accompaniments,' was the answer. They looked into and under the piano, then in every room and closet in the house; examined the windows and outbuildings—but no one was to be found. They took off the lid of the piano to see if a mouse could have set it to playing, or to see if a music box could have been hidden within it; searched everywhere in vain for the performer. The following night it was the same, and so on for several nights in succession. Neighbors were called in, and declared that the parlor was haunted. The servants left the house in fear. Still the grand Steinway awoke the inmates of the house nightly with its dulcet tones. The keys could be seen moving up and down, while marches, quicksteps, bits of operas followed each other in rapid succession—

now swelling like martial music, grand and glorious; again dying away to a whisper, then rising like the sound of a storm or furious battle.

"The first intimation we had of their parlor being haunted was when its owner asked Mr. Doree if his piano ever got out of order and played right on, of its own accord, and, when answered in the negative, told us why he had asked the question. He acknowledged that he was greatly puzzled—said he could give no solution to the mystery. He remarked that the keys were certainly manipulated by 'invisible fingers.' Then, after a silence of a few minutes: 'The strangest part of it is that neither my sister nor myself are able to play this class of music, which we recognize as the work of the old masters, and the servants cannot tell one note from another. Our neighbors are unable to whistle a single bar of it, let alone playing it. There is not another instrument of the kind on our street. My sister thought that some wag had hidden a music box inside of the piano, but we have had it taken all apart, had it tuned over anew and searched everywhere, but found nothing. It plays beautifully such music as I have heard my late wife play on her father's piano.'

"'Well,' I said, 'it is clear that the house is haunted. It would hardly be safe for you if we were living in the witch-burning age.' He laughed rather nervously, I fancied, and said, 'Good night, come and hear it for yourselves,' and we went.

"He told my husband's partner the same story. All the people in the town declared that his dead wife had come back to punish him for not buying her an instrument, while the more malicious gossips of the town said that 'there must have been *foul play* in the manner of Mrs. Butterfield's death.' There was talk of lynching the young widower—of disinterring his poor wife's remains, and every one was for avenging her wrongs, when he suddenly closed his house, sold his effects, including the haunted piano, and sent his sister back to England."

"Well, does the instrument still entertain its new owners?"

"Oh, no! That is the oddest part of the whole story. The lady who owns it has never been disturbed by any nocturnal music. The ghost has stopped playing. No invisible spirit hands now touch the keys. Both herself and daughters play very unscientifically. If poor Alice did return, she did so to punish her cruel husband and no one else. He is still boarding at the hotel uptown, but it is rumored that he will soon marry Pansy's nurse. Some people are yet suspicious of his neglect, of possible *foul play* in his wife's last sickness, but Dr. Webb is a Christian gentleman, whose veracity has rarely been doubted, and his testimony ought to be believed, I suppose. He affirms that the poor lady was delirious and destroyed her own life; that the husband went to him in great distress of mind and begged him, the doctor, to save the sick woman, if possible. Of course, Mr. Butterfield or any other man would not half-commit a deed of that kind and stand the chance of being exposed by the victim and brought to trial, if not to the gallows," she added.

"No—that certainly is in his favor. If he alone had heard the music we might have accounted for it on the score of a haunted conscience; but, as others heard it, one does not know what to think of it," I said. *"But who was the musician?"*

"Little Pansy is now four years old. She is still under the care of her nurse," said Mrs. Doree. I subsequently heard the same story from a number of the town's people, and have given it to the reader as it was told to me, unmodified in any particular.

CHAPTER XIV.

IRRESISTIBLE IMPULSE.

An irresistible impulse to write to a friend, or make an unpremeditated visit, or to postpone an intended journey, because something seemed to say, "You must not go," we have all experienced. To illustrate my meaning, I will relate a true occurrence. A gentleman, after engaging his stateroom for an ocean voyage, postponed his journey for a fortnight, because he had a startling impression that he should not sail in a certain vessel. The ship was run down by a tramp steamer and nearly all on board perished. A week later he set sail on another ocean liner and landed at Havre in safety. But why did not all on the doomed boat have a similar warning?

During the great Centennial Fair I started with my sister one morning for the Quaker City. An irresistible impulse to return home, after we had reached the station and were just stepping into the car, caused my sister to exclaim: "Stop! I must go home! We will take the next train." It was vain to urge her to go then, and she went home. As she entered the house the maid handed her a valuable ring which she had found on the breakfast table, and said: "I was afraid you would come back for it and lose your train." "Yes," said my sister, "there it goes now, but we will take the next one."

We went back to the station and the agent said:

"It was fortunate that you did not take the early train, for it was wrecked at G——, a dozen miles below us, and many of the excursionists were killed and wounded."

"Now I know why I *had* to go home," said my sister; "it was truly a Providential impression which caused our delay this morning, for everything was all right at my home."

We reached the city of Philadelphia in safety, thanks to an over-ruling Providence. But the wreck of the morning train was the worst during the Centennial Exposition.

Martin Luther felt an irresistible impulse to fling his inkstand at the devil. Did he see the devil with his mortal eyes? Does everybody experience such sensations? What is irresistible impulse? Is it a temptation from the evil one—or a germ of latent insanity? Or of suicidal mania? Or the whisper of a spirit?

Scientists have failed to give a lucid explanation. Mental philosophy does not clearly explain why a man will yield to an uncontrollable desire to place his hand under the falling hammer on an anvil or jump from the Brooklyn Bridge. I have never been able to explain why I cannot stand upon the deck of a ship or in front of a coming steam engine, or above the rapids of Niagara, on a high tower, or above the roaring machinery in the iron rolling mills, without feeling an almost irresistible impulse to fling myself down. And this desire is always without any known motive. If there is a latent desire to experience the awful sensation of falling, of being ground to atoms beneath ponderous machinery, or of being hurled by a boiling maelstrom of relentless, hungry waters into eternity, and in one breathless moment to realize a waking nightmare, I know not; for I cannot analayze my feelings at such a time. My whole being seems to be wrapped up in the sublimity, of the awful height, or power, or grandeur of the scene beneath my eyes. Fear is for the time dead. A sort of fiendish exaltation holds possession of my mind, nerves and brain; yes, every particle of my flesh is alive with this awful longing to make the fatal plunge. Did Christ experience this desire to fling himself down, I wonder, when he was tempted by Beelzebub on that high mountain? Or did he see the tempter in person? Is this desire the origin of suicidal mania? Again, where does this unnatural impulse end? Medical experts tell us that it is not insanity, for every one is, at times, subject to such impulsions, and they reason that if it is a mania, then that all men are monomaniacs, more or less; that it would be impossible to draw the line between the sane and insane. But, be this true or false reasoning, I ask again, where does this so-called *irresistible impulse* end? Do you answer, *In self-destruction?* Do you remind me of the recent case of the boy murderer who, when on trial, declared that his desire *to kill* was too strong for his powers of resistance—that he *"had* to kill" his victims—that he took their innocent lives because, in his own words, he *"had to do it?"*

A few months ago a man leaped from the top floor of a foundry into a caldron of burning or liquid iron, in my native State.

From the Trenton *Advertiser*, October 5, 1884, I copy the following extract of a letter from Bradford, Pa., dated October 4, 1884. It says: "A day or two ago a tall, handsome woman got into the ladies' car at Dunkirk. With her was a bright little boy, some two years old. The child laughed and played with the passengers. When the train left Cataragus the woman who seemed nervous, got out of her seat, picked up the baby and started for the rear of the car.

"A short distance east of Cataragus is a long, deep gulf, over which the cars run over a high trestle. The distance from the top of the trestle to the wagon road below is perhaps one hundred feet. A sharp and short curve leads to it. As the train rushed over the gulf a woman's piercing shriek was heard. 'I looked,' said the brakeman, 'and saw an object leap from the platform into the rocky gulf. That object, sir, was the lady passenger; and in her arms, closely pressed to her breast, was her infant. I pulled the bell cord and the train came to a halt. How it happened I cannot say, but at the time the woman jumped a load of hay, drawn by a pair of oxen, passed under the trestle. Mother and child landed squarely in the centre of the hay and were thus saved from a horrible death. The woman, who was not hurt in the least, said her name was Mrs. Adam Schell, and her home was in Michigan. She was on her way to visit friends in the oil country.' Mrs. Schell said that she could not explain her action. When near the car door she was seized with an insane desire to jump from the train." I should call the above an excellent illustration of irresistible impulse.

Is not the suicidal mania an irresistible impulse?

I have somewhere seen a painting by a celebrated artist, in which the central figure was a noble-looking youth. On his right was an angel whispering in his ear, on his left a fiend endeavoring to lead him astray. Is the old artist's idea true? Are these morbid impulses the suggestions of the evil spirit, and do our good impressions and desires and monitions come from our guardian angels? Are conscience and desire, which sway us like reeds in the gale and lead us into good or evil against our own will power, only suggestions from guardian angels or lost spirits? Again, has not the Holy Spirit been sent into the world since the age of prophecy and miracles *"to reprove the world of sin, and of righteousness, and of judgment,"* also, to *"guide"* us *"into all truth?"* And will not this Holy Spirit save us from self-destruction, from the suggestions of the soul's worst enemy, if we open the ears of our hearts and receive His teachings?

May irresistible impulse belong to, or be a product of, habit? Habits of unbridled thoughts and actions and idle day dreams may lead the soul astray. Habit cannot be classed among the natural attributes of individuals. It is always something *acquired.*

Our spiritual, intellectual and physical natures form a trinity. Give the first, or emotional, full reins, and it runs into melancholia, or religious mania. Allow the second full sway, and we have insanity. Leave the third, or animal, tendency unchecked by conscience, reason, human laws or Divine love, and lo! instead of the noblest work of God, behold a brute—an orang-outang or chimpanzee!

We are all monomaniacs to a greater or less degree. Is not habit itself a sort of mania, a species of insanity? May not the practice of drinking spirituous liquors, of chewing, smoking or snuffing tobacco, drinking tea and coffee to excess, as well as eating morphia, hachesh, quinine, camphor, caffeine, arsenic, and using chloral, be classed with other kinds of mania?

Cannot an unnatural craving for certain beverages or edibles be called a habit? The practice of contracting debts, of gambling, betting, using profane language, of carelessness in dress, or in speaking one's mother tongue, also of indulging in slang phrases and obscene expressions, has, in all instances, been acquired, and may consequently be classed with the manias or bad habits.

It is always easier to fall into a habit than to correct it. Personal habits, like evil thoughts, run in certain grooves or brain cells. "Doing good deeds, aiding the poor, visiting the sick, praying or attending church regularly, may," says a writer on psychology, "be classed as habits."

Some have a *penchant* for making collections of plants, insects, marine curiosities or minerals; birds, pictures, china and bric-a-brac; stamps and autographs, or rare books, Indian relics and implements of warfare. Sleeplessness, soliloquizing, somnambulism, loquacity, gossiping, exaggerating, as well as seeing spectres and being subject to singular hallucinations or victims to suicidal mania, kleptomania or irresistible impulses, may, I should suppose, be classed as habits.

Imagination, glorious and indispensable gift to mortals, may be so unduly cultured that its possessor may be accused of drifting into all kinds of absurd isms, if not dementias.

May not the various forms of insanity, also of seeing ghosts, be attributed to diseased or overtrained imagination? Or, does the victim of superstition allow his thoughts to dwell upon the *unknown* until, like the Witch of Endor, he can summon at will all sorts of hobgoblins? Were those who were possessed of evil spirits in Christ's time simply insane, or were they suffering from diseased imaginations, or were they really possessed of devils? Is that the case of the insane to-day? And if devils or evil spirits can enter the minds of human beings still, what is to hinder spirits, good or bad, from appearing in visible form in the twentieth century?

CHAPTER XV.

THE PHANTOM CHILD.

I FIRST met Mrs. Lura Linwell at Sea Beach, where for several years I spent my annual vacations, and we soon became the best of friends. She had a horse and carriage and we often took long drives together along the sandy beach and through the beautiful country.

During one of our pleasant outings she told me the following pathetic story, which I will give in her own words, without any comments:

"I married the man of my choice, and we were very happy for five years, before I was blessed with a little daughter. My husband said then that our happiness was complete, and for a season our joy knew no shadow. It was enough to know that the great blessing of motherhood was mine, but as she grew older and evinced great aptitude for learning, my pride in her knew no bounds. She became my sole charge. I would not trust my darling to the care of a nurse even, and my husband became second to her in my affections.

"As I have said, little May was very precocious. Her memory was wonderful. She had a natural gift for elocution and music. At the age of three years she could spell, read, recite and sing better than many children of double her years. How proud I was of my darling! I resolved to educate her myself. Oh, what plans I made for her! I shut myself up in my study whenever

I could leave the nursery, and spent my time in reviewing my studies. I had professors in French, music, Latin and painting, and, as the years went on, reviewed the entire preparatory course for college, because I shrank from the idea of sending her away from home to finish her education. She was a nervous, frail-looking child, but I was deaf to the warnings of my husband and callers, for I was deceived by the brightness of her eyes and the unnatural flush on her cheeks, which I took for the hue of health, and daily rejoiced in her rapid progress.

"I had formerly been extravagantly fond of society, but since the hope of motherhood had dawned upon my mind had completely given up making calls, going to balls, parties, theatres or the opera. I even refused to see my society friends when they called during May's infancy, or to leave her long enough to attend church. My husband demurred—deprecated the entire change in my tastes and mode of living. He declared that the cares of maternity had robbed him of my affection and companionship—made me neglect all other claims upon my time, but I was deaf to his remonstrances. The only drawback to my happiness was my impatience. I was not satisfied with the child's unnatural attainments.

"She was in great demand at musicales and children's entertainments, as well as the Demorest Contests. At the age of six years she had ably won the silver and small gold medals, as well as the W. C. T. U. musical medals, both silver and gold. Had she lived she would have become a great songstress, as well as a celebrated elocutionist—but 'God's ways are not our ways.'

"How I prided myself on her wonderful memory, for she played and sang both by note and from memory with exquisite taste, expression and precision. As usual, little May had been invited to sing at a concert which was being given in the Academy of Music for the benefit of the public library in our home city. She had succeeded grandly during the early part of the performance and received an encore which would have rendered a professional adult proud of her laurels. As the evening was drawing to a close May was called to sing the final number. I shall never cease to see her, as she stood there in her white lace frock, adorned with a necklace of medals, her long, golden curls falling like a veil around her white neck and shoulders, 'perfect even to the white kid slippers,' her father whispered, as her beautiful voice swelled sweetly through the hall, filling it with silvery music.

"The large audience listened, spellbound, to her clear, pure tones, and I could almost hear the beating of my own heart as I marked the spiritual beauty of her face and the brightness of her large, blue eyes, when she suddenly paused in the beginning of the third stanza and sank fainting to the platform.

"Kindly hands carried her to the vestibule and placed her limp form in my arms. She did not recover consciousness for hours. Convulsions followed, and for two days she hovered over the brink of the grave. You can imagine my sorrow.

"On the second night after her attack she suddenly awoke, started up in bed and exclaimed: 'Mamma! I remember the rest of my song!' Then in sweet, unearthly tones she sang:

> "'One eve a light shone round her bed
> And there she saw him stand,
> Her infant in his little shroud,
> A taper in his hand.

"Oh, mother, see! my shroud is dry,
And I can sleep once more!"
And, beautiful, the parting smile,
The little infant wore,'

then fell back on her pillow and—died.

"For weeks after her death I was almost delirious. I refused to see the minister, my friends, even my almost broken-hearted husband, and nursed my grief in silence. Conscience was at work. I knew that my inordinate ambition had killed my darling. My husband's affection appeared to be hopelessly estranged. His sad, stern face and silence were reproof enough, although he refrained from reproaches.

"My only relief was in visiting her grave. Every day I went to the cemetery, covered her grave with flowers and spent hours sitting there, weeping and praying for pardon for my great sin in not listening to reason and the advice of friends.

"A long, cold storm came on and continued for days, for it was late in October, and I remained in my room, thinking of her lying in her chill, damp bed beneath the dripping rain, until I feared that my reason would be dethroned; while my husband paced the library alone, or sat with his head bowed over the study table, but I did not believe that he was grieving for our child.

"One night, as I sat weeping and thinking of her sweet face and form in her dark, damp bed, I suddenly looked up and saw my darling standing near me, all white and shining, and smiling as if in life and health. I stretched out my hands to clasp her to my bosom, but she seemed to recede towards the door, and said:

"'Come, dear mamma. We will go and comfort poor papa.

He is crying all alone in the library,' waving her hand toward the door and gliding noiselessly into the hall. I followed her through the hall, downstairs and into the library. She looked back, still smiling and beckoning me on, till she stood beside her father's chair. His head was bowed upon the table, and I saw by the convulsive movements of his shoulders that he was weeping as only a strong man can weep.

"I went to him and whispered: 'Dear Frank, here is our little May!'

He looked up in a dazed sort of way and asked: 'Where is she?'

"'Here,' I said, pointing to her, 'she has come to comfort us,' but as he looked again she vanished like a moonbeam when a cloud steals over the moon and as silently.

"'Why, Lura, you have been dreaming,' Frank said, as he took my hand and led me from the room. 'But what made you think our dead darling was with me?'

"I told him. Still holding my arm, he turned on the gas in the corridors and in all of the rooms on the first and second floors, but she was nowhere to be seen.

"'You have surely been dreaming, Lura!' he said again, after we had reached my room. I answered:

"'If it was a dream, Frank, I slept all the way to the library.'

'Dear little phantom child!' he said, 'I wish I had seen you!'

"I told him what she had said. It seemed to comfort him, for after a long silence he declared that we would, hereafter, bear our sorrows in each other's company, and not selfishly shut ourselves up alone with our grief, but share it, as well as our joy, together. He further said that he had not dared to intrude upon me with his presence. That the child's death had almost killed *him,* as well as myself. It cut me to the heart to think how selfish I had been and I asked his pardon.

"He put his arms around me tenderly, and from that time we were more closely drawn together in sympathy for our common pursuits than ever before, and love each other better than during the first years of our married life.

"Other children—a boy six years old and a girl four years—bless our home. They are strong, healthy, romping playmates, and not at all precocious; indeed, have not yet been taught the alphabet, but they shall enter a kindergarten next year. So, you see, they are not likely to be injured by too much early training. They are with their nurse in the country this summer, at the home of their grandmother.

"You are welcome to use this story in any way you please. If you have it published I hope you will name it *The Phantom Child.* It may be a warning to parents who tax the frail organisms of their little ones beyond their strength.

"But tell me what you think I saw? Was it an apparition, an optical illusion or a dream?"

And I had to answer:

"I think it was a *dream,* superinduced by your allowing your mind to dwell so persistently upon your bereavement. Perhaps it was sent by the angel of your little translated child to show you your duty to your husband. You know it is said in 'Holy Writ' *that in heaven their angels do always behold the face of the* FATHER. If it was a sleeping or waking vision, or if you were in a clairvoyant state I am sure the vision was sent for your good. It may have been an optical illusion, caused by over-tasked brain and nerves and loss of sleep. But I am inclined to believe that you walked in your sleep till you reached your husband's side, dreaming all the way."

I answered, I fear, rather cruelly, adding, "But I thank you for the story of the 'Phantom Child.' The reader will perceive that I could not here take refuge in agnosticism."

CHAPTER XVI.

A DREAM WARNING.

DREAMS often come as warnings. A very singular one haunted my sleeping hours for years.

The scene was a strip of meadow land on both sides of a deep, slow-moving creek, now swollen to a river so wide that it covered all of the field and stretched away into the woodland beyond. During the spring freshet it appeared like a shallow lake as far as the eye could reach. An unfinished piece of stone wall on the right bank of the stream stretched a distance of about ten rods along the bank, but in my dream picture the water was flowing over each end of the wall and beyond it, as well as on both sides. The ice had apparently been broken up by the recent rains, for it was floating all over the surface of the water in small cakes. The water between the bits of ice was muddy. There was not a spot on the whole visible lakelet where one could walk, or swim, or sail a boat.

In the centre of the half-sunken wall I always saw a lone figure, that of a woman. She was poorly clad, thin in flesh, but her face I recognized as *my own*. She was always pale, and her eyes were tearless, but the stony, hopeless expression of her countenance told of despair, of a famishing soul, as well as body. At the first glance I always said in my dream: "She is going to commit suicide," but when I saw her turn to the right and left anxiously, as if trying to see some way of escape, for the water was still rising and the night fast settling down over wave and woodland, I knew that some fiend had lured her there against her will to destroy herself. Then, oddly enough, instead of being a spectator, I appeared to be the principal actor of the drama. My own form seemed to be merged into that of the lone woman who had been standing in such utter despair and desolation upon that piece of wall which was already submerged by the rising water. Darkness soon covered the earth. The waves rose higher and higher. They had reached her (my) feet, anon my neck. Human aid was out of the question, for there was neither house nor living being within sight or hearing of that gruesome place. The icy water kissed my lips, then lifted me from the wall. I tried to cling to a cake of floating ice, but failed. A numbness stole over me, but consciousness was wide awake. A horror of the unknown took possession of my mind as I was whirled over the falls into—nothingness, but I awoke as I sank, to find that it was *only a dream*. The same vision was repeated again and again for seven years.

It was, to me, an unaccountable one, as I had never been placed in a like situation, although I had often seen the bit of unfinished wall above described and the field and wood covered with water and floating ice during the spring and autumn freshets.

Here comes the solution of my frightful dream.

The scene described above is a portion of our old plantation.

The unfinished wall and swollen stream form the dividing line between the main farm and an eight-acre lot which my father purchased only a few years before his death. He had paid for this land and received a good warrantee deed, as he then supposed. The deed had been duly recorded in the country archives, and up to this time, seven years from my first Dream of Desolation, nobody had disputed his right to the new lot of land.

Two or three years after my father's death my mother sold the whole of her farm to a gentleman from Newark. The purchaser agreed to pay half of the money down, and the remainder six months later or forfeit $5,000, and his attorney compelled my mother to sign a paper as follows: "I agree to give the second party a *clear* title for the number of acres specified, or forfeit the sum of $5,000 if I fail to fulfill my part of the above contract." A foolish thing to do. During the months which intervened between the signing of the above contract and the consummation of the sale of said property, my Dream of Desolation, as I mentally called it, was almost nightly repeated. I would find myself dreaming or wondering at my vision while on the railway or in stage coaches. When the day approached on which we were to furnish the deed and receive the purchase money the lawyer who had been employed by the second party informed us that there was a defect in the title of the new piece of land *where the scene of my dream was laid,* also, that under these circumstances my mother would be obliged to forfeit the amount above named in the contract she had so foolishly signed or make the title good. The purchaser was inclined, at first, to take advantage, but finally agreed to give us a few days' time to enable us to get another deed from the original owner, who was an octogenarian, and had moved into another State.

While we were awaiting her action the New York City gentleman proposed for my hand. "If you will marry me I'll burn the contract and let that eight-acre bit of worthless swamp go. Besides this, I will give your mother a home for life on the old homestead," he said, "for I am a rich man and a widower." I opened my eyes and looked at him coolly. "Is it possible that he had known of the defective title to the swamp lot before he attempted to purchase our land?" I asked myself. "You will never be sorry," he added, "for I have a beautiful place in the city. I will build a summer residence here, and give you *carte blanche* for beautifying the grounds and your father's grave"—there is a family cemetery on the old farm—"so you had better consent."

"Of course, I should be glad to give my mother a good home and decorate my father's grave, but—no. This man is a villain. I cannot do myself such an injustice," I thought. But how to get out of the lion's jaws was the question. I had dreamed of living in the great City of New York all my life. To have my dear mother with me will be delightful—and she always loved the old place. I am weary of my past and present life of struggle; why not accept a home and fortune?" I asked myself, when, suddenly, like a flash of lightning, came the oft-repeated dream into my mind. Clear and distinct as I had dreamed it a hundred times, I saw myself standing there alone, my pale, hopeless face outlined against the fading western sky—a desolate, all-alone figure in the midst of death, of despair, with nothing earthly to cling to except those slippery masses of floating ice.

Yes, as if by an electric flashlight, all the perceptive powers of my soul were suddenly illumined, and I realized for the first time the full interpretation of my oft-repeated vision. With all his wealth and opportunities for mind culture, my would-be lover was an illiterate, vulgar, unsympathetic man. United to him in marriage I would have stood as much alone, in as utter desolation, as the woman in my vision, and my whole soul cried "No!"

But one must give Cerberas his cake, and I asked for a week's delay. A favorable reply with the correct signature to the deed arrived soon afterward, and I gave him a *negative answer*. My dream never returned after that affair was settled. I now know that my good angel had for years been trying to tell me to look up that defective title, also to warn me against a future where I would have stood as entirely alone as I did in my vision; and I shall never cease to thank God for my warning, in the shape of a dream. The above is a true story, *my own bona-fide* experience, and I have never felt any qualms of conscience for counterplotting against the villain who would have ruined my mother financially, for I am still convinced that he knew all about that defective title *before he drew up the contract.*

CHAPTER XVII.

DREAMS FULFILLED.

"Are your dreams ever fulfilled?"

"Yes, my dreams are often fulfilled," said a well-known Pennsylvania lady in answer to my question.

"More than twenty years ago," she added, "I dreamed of taking a journey to a far country—somewhere toward the setting sun—where I saw beautiful scenery, high, snow-capped mountains, flowery valleys and wonderful forests. I traveled in railway coaches, in stages and then sailed upon a stormy ocean in an elegant steamer, but was finally left on a desolate pier in mid-ocean, alone.

"Years passed on, till the dream, which had at first made such a deep impression on my mind, was forgotten. A score of years after its occurrence I went quite unexpectedly, to myself, to California. We took the overland route. My first view of the Rocky Mountains recalled my long-lost dream. I shall never forget how familiar the mountains, valleys, wild flowers, great trees, as well as the scenery along the Pacific coast, appeared to me. Indeed, it was not new to me at all. I had seen it all, twenty years earlier, in a vision of the night; yet it seemed as if I had passed over the same route but yesterday.

"We landed on the new pier at Santa Barbara, but found to our dismay that a portion of the pier near the shore *was gone.* That the old pier, which had carelessly been left standing after the new one was built, had drifted against the shore end of the new one and torn it away during a gale on the previous night. What to do we knew not. To land was clearly impossible, for the surf was so high that no small boat could live, while the steamer could not venture any nearer to the dangerous shoals. The captain gave us our choice, namely, to go a hundred miles further down the coast before landing, or to remain on the pier until the sea was calm enough for small boats to breast the breakers and take us to the land. We foolishly chose the latter, supposing that the pier was perfectly safe, but had to remain there, in imminent peril of being swept out to sea, *for eighteen hours!* If ever a dream was fulfilled, mine was."

I remember another prophetic dream. I crossed a muddy river and just as I reached the opposite side saw a child's red stockings and little shoes under the end of the bridge. A little further down the stream, I dreamed, that a man was standing in a boat, weeping bitterly, and looking at a dark object in the water.

I had nearly forgotten my dream, when one day I went with my aunt across the Paupack River to gather cranberries. Just as we reached the opposite side of the stream I saw a pair of shoes and stockings. In an instant my dream flashed across my mind. I looked hurriedly down the river and saw a man in a boat crying and wringing his hands. "What is the matter?" I asked. "I am looking for my little boy, who was drowned," he answered, "but I cannot see him." He waded across the river here, and that is the last we have seen of him. I looked down into the water as he finished speaking and saw the body of his little son lying there within a few feet of me. The child was dead. Here was the sequel of my dream. The place, the scene, the man in the boat, the dark object—his son's corpse—in the bottom of the river, and the little fellow's shoes and red stockings under the bridge! This is as true as the Gospel.

The wife of a Methodist clergyman says: "Three years ago, while my husband was attending the annual conference, I dreamed that the Bishop had sent us to Schenevas, N. Y., for the coming year. The next morning I told my son that I knew where we were going.

"'Where?' he asked. I told him. 'Why, mother, when did you hear?' he asked. I told him I had dreamed it.

"That evening my son met his father at the station and asked where we were going to live next year?

"'To Schenevas,' was the answer.

"'Why, that is just where mother dreamed we were going to be sent, father,' said Albert. 'Isn't it funny?' 'Yes, I should call that a prophetic dream,' rejoined his father."

Not more than a month ago a lady celebrated for her piety and devotion to her family told me the following dream, in reply to my question, whether any of her dreams were ever fulfilled:

"You will remember my little Mary? She was a sweet, engaging child, my idol, and the pet of the household. She was my only daughter. I was so fearful that harm would come to my darling that I rarely ever allowed her out of my sight, day or night. She was a playful, healthy, little fairy, and my friends all said was wise beyond her years. One night I dreamed that I saw her lying in a coffin with her head severed entirely from her body. I awoke with an hysterical scream, and my joy as well as thankfulness knew no bounds when I found my little Mary safe and well. She was still asleep, but there was a happy smile on her sweet lips, and her dimpled cheeks glowed with the color of health.

"My terrified scream had awakened my husband. 'What is the matter?' he asked. I told him. 'Why, that is strange,' he said, 'I had the same dream only a few nights ago, but was afraid to tell you about it. I am almost certain that something is going to happen to our child.'

"Mary died a few days later. She *choked to death with the croup*. I have always thought that our dream was sent to warn us of her death," my friend added.

"But her head was not cut off," I said.

"No, yet it might as well have been, for all the good it did the poor child. You know, the disease was all in her throat. Twenty years have gone by since that night of agony, yet I am still unable to speak of her sufferings with calmness. Our joint dream that she was dead came to pass, at least," she answered, "and must have been a warning."

Mrs. W——, aged about sixty, a widow of good standing in my native town, says: "After my husband died I sold our farm and stock on six months' credit, with good security. One night I dreamed that my deceased husband came to me and said: 'Sally, those vendue notes will be due in three days, when those who secured them will have a chance to withdraw their names. See to them at once, or you will lose a good deal of money.' His appearance so frightened me that I awoke and went to my desk, examined the notes, which I had not thought were so nearly due, and found everything just as he had told me in my dream. But for this timely warning I *should* have lost considerable money, I presume."

A widow lady called on me this morning on business. Without knowing that I was writing or had ever written a word on this subject, for she is a stranger in this place, she told me the following dream:

"I am a widow, the mother of three small children," she said, "and am in quite destitute circumstances. The loss of his property, through no fault of his own, compelled my husband to leave his family and go West in order to redeem his fortune. He was an excellent mechanic and soon found remunerative work in the city of Leadville. I received a check for fifty dollars from him monthly for over a year. We were looking forward to a reunion with him in Leadville, when a letter came, stating that he was *en route* for the City of Mexico. 'I can get much higher wages there,' he wrote. 'Will write as soon as I reach my destination.'

"About a week later I was suddenly awakened from a dream, in which I heard his voice and step and peculiar rap on my chamber door. I sprang out of bed and listened, then opened the door, but there was no one there. I ran out into the hall, then downstairs and opened the front door, but all was as silent as the grave. Only the cold moon and stars seemed to be awake. As I went upstairs I met my eldest child in the passage. 'Has papa come?' he asked. 'I heard him call you, mamma, before you went downstairs,' he added. I went back to bed in a dazed sort of way, thinking to myself, 'I have been dreaming.' When I finally slept again I dreamed that there was a railway collision—then parties were fighting and I saw my husband's body cut up into small pieces and put into a box. I awoke in a great fright, for I then knew that he was dead. My fears were confirmed soon after. He had been killed by some cowboys in Mexico. I have called to see if you can aid me in any way," added the destitute widow.

Fifty Thousand Dollars Saved by a Dream in Minnesota.

A gentleman who has long been cashier in a well-known bank received $50,000 one day, just after the vaults were closed for the night. He carried the money to his home, and deposited it in a safe, without mentioning the fact to any member of his family. He dreamed that a burglar was getting into his chamber through the window, and sprang up in bed in such haste as to awaken his wife, who exclaimed: "I dreamed that burglars were getting into our room. Light the gas, quick, and see if the windows and doors are fastened!"

"Judge of our surprise," continued the cashier, "on finding that a large pane of glass had been cut out of our bay window; also, that a ladder was leaning against the casement. The safe had not been opened, but for our timely dream not only the money, but our lives might have been taken. The burglars must have heard me spring out of bed in time to make good their escape while my wife was telling her dream. Our daughter had a similar vision the same night, only varied by seeing masked men breaking open my safe. Since that time I have believed in the theory of guardian angels."

The above was the experience of a Christian gentleman, whose word is as good as a bond. Should it ever be necessary he will give his affidavit to corroborate this story.

"My husband," said a lady, "believes in dreams. A few years ago he dreamed that he was out hunting in a certain well-known forest, and found a bee tree. The next day he told his dream to some friends, who urged him to go and see if such a tree could be found, then offered to accompany him. They went on the following day to the scene described in his dream, where they found the bee tree, exactly as my husband had seen it in his dream two nights before. Now, how did this knowledge come to him? He had not been in the woods where the tree was found in twenty years, at the time of his dream. They came back with their pails full of choice honey."

My maternal grandmother often related the following dream. She was an intelligent old lady, and her memory was unimpaired, although she was eighty-five years of age. Her early home was in Morristown, N. J. Her father was a deacon in the Presbyterian Church and his daughter had been educated in the same faith. She was an only daughter, but there were five sons. After her brothers were all grown to manhood the deacon purchased a large tract of land in Pennsylvania and gave a hundred acres of it to each of his sons. Some years after the young men had settled on their land their father died. Their sister had married a poor man from New York City. She was living in the same neighborhood with her brothers, on a rented farm, which, they told her, had belonged to the original tract of land owned by her late father. She said that she often wondered why her father had left his sons well off in this world's goods, but made no provision for her. She used to weep over her altered fortunes, for she had been brought up in a home of plenty, and wished her father back again that she might demand her share of his property.

"If the farm on which we lived had only been ours we could have got along finely, but it took all we could make on it to pay the rent each year. Then I had to spin and weave and make our own clothing, besides," grandmother said, "so you see, it is no wonder that I fretted and felt that I had not received my own, or that I daily thought how unjust it was that my brothers should all have been left rich and I so poor.

"One night, while thinking over my hard lot, for I worked like a slave to feed and clothe my large family of (fourteen) children, I fell asleep and dreamed that my father came into my bedroom and sat down on a large, old-fashioned chest which had once been his. I told him I was glad he had come back, for I wanted to ask him what I had done that had caused him to forget me so long, and why he had not left me a farm as well as my brothers? Then, with his old, kind smile, he told me that the farm on which we then lived was mine—that he had deeded it to me just before his death. 'Your brother Jacob holds the deed for you,' he said; 'ask him about it—see to it at once.'

"I dreamed the same dream three times that night. The next day I went to my brother Jacob's. He was not in, so I told his wife all about my vision. 'Well, Mary,' Phoebe said, 'your dream is true. Jacob and his brothers know all about it. They are only keeping the home for you, for fear your husband might sell it and leave you homeless. You had better be quiet and help them keep the secret. It was your father's wish.' It was all true. Jacob gave me the deed and told me it was recorded in my name only the year before. After that," said grandma, "I always had great faith in dreams."

"But what became of the rent money?" I asked.

"Oh, he saved it for a rainy day," she said, "for me."

"I always heard, grandma, that you had only ten children."

"You are right. The four oldest of the family were step-children, but I had to care for them, just the same," was the reply. "Your grandfather never would stay long in any one place, and afterward persuaded me to sell my farm and go to the Lake Country," she added. So her dream did her no great good except to save her father from censure. *But it was fulfilled.*

Many of my own dreams have been fulfilled. When I was about ten years of age my father presented an ornamental comb to me. It was large enough to reach almost around my head and was just the thing to keep the refractory curls out of my eyes. Of course, I was very proud of my beautiful gift, and I well remember standing a long time before the old-fashioned looking-glass admiring its effect before I laid it away and prepared for sleep.

I dreamed that night that my mother, or some one else, boxed my ears and broke my pretty comb. I awoke crying. The next day I was so unfortunate as to break one of the rules of school—I believe it was the one about whispering—when my teacher came up behind me and boxed my ears soundly. My pretty comb was broken into three pieces by her brutal blow, thus literally fulfilling my dream of the previous night.

I remember a dream in which I saw a neighbor's funeral procession leave his residence. A week later he died very suddenly and I saw my recent dream repeated exactly in reality.

I used to pride myself on my success in teaching algebra, but one day a problem in a new edition which I had not examined refused to come right. I tried it again and again, but at 4 o'clock was no nearer its solution than I had been in the morning. I went home and worked at it until midnight, but with the same result. At length, wearied out with my unusual mental excitement, I fell asleep and *dreamed it all out* so clearly that, upon awakening I sprang out of bed and worked out my problem exactly as I had dreamed of doing, and found to my delight that the result was correct.

Sometimes our sins find us out and haunt us for long years afterward in the shape of dreams. I recollect one neglect of duty which has troubled my slumbers for three decades. I was some ten or fifteen minutes late a few times during my teaching days in my last school, and, in order to get through with my classes at the regular hour for closing, put off calling the roll until a more convenient time, when I would mark the attendance from memory. A bad plan, you will say. Certainly, and not always correct. The result of this dereliction of duty, although unknown to any one except myself, haunts me still. Whenever I am tired or ill I dream of being late to school, of not calling the attendance roll *for a whole month,* and awake in terror for fear the directors or principal will find how careless I have been in not making out my monthly report correctly.

One night, while a thousand miles from home, I dreamed that every member of my family except myself was at my eldest brother's house. There was a long procession of carriages outside, into which I saw my friends seat themselves, but I could not see my brother.

As the last carriage left the door I heard little Frank, my brother's two-year-old baby, cry:

"Papa, papa! Let me go with my papa. Don't put papa in a box!"

My brother died a week later, but I did not hear of his death till after my return to his home, when I also was told that poor baby Frank screamed and called for his father (exactly as I had dreamed) when the remains were carried out of the house and placed in the hearse.

If you make a study of dream life you will find that dreams fulfilled are not rare occurrences. Prophetic dreams have been common in all ages.

CHAPTER XVIII.

A VISION OF HEAVEN.

I ONCE had a vision of heaven. It may not have been the one described by St. John in the Apocalypse, but it was a place so glorious that, if I fail to behold it again, when this mortal shall have put on immortality, my soul will be cruelly disappointed and heaven will not be heaven. That glimpse or foretaste of the beatitudes occurred when I was but little above childhood, soon after the death of my most intimate girl friend; but its beauty, like her lovely features, will never fade from my recollection. She had visited me but a few days previous to her sudden, but brief, illness, and we had a wild, joyous time. When we said "good-bye" under the apple blossoms we little thought that this was to be our last earthly meeting; yet in less than a fortnight Lina was lying in her coffin. The sudden news of her death so entirely prostrated me that I was unable to attend the funeral, but I visited her grave a few days later and covered it with wild roses, azaleas and dogwood blossoms, fit emblems of the one who slumbered there so peacefully. It did not seem possible that the little mound I had decorated contained all that I had loved and admired in my lost companion. "Why is it," I mournfully cried, "that the fairest flowers are the first to fade, that the lovely and gifted ones of earth die before they have half fulfilled the promise of their early years, that 'death loves a shining mark?'" But the wind and rustling leaves alone seemed to listen to my earnest inquiries, and I bowed my head upon her grave in an agony of weeping.

That night I had the following dream, or, rather, vision, for our so-called dreams are often *visions:*

I was dead. My lifeless body was lying in a casket awaiting the hour of burial. Weeping friends stood around, gazing sorrowfully upon my dead face, which was so soon to be consigned to the tomb, and hidden forever from earthly eyes.

My spirit, which had assumed a new and glorious form, was also present, although invisible to mourning relatives, and, like them, was taking leave of "this earthly tabernacle;" yet, unlike them, wondering why any one could sorrow for its release from the diseased, pain-laden body, which had so long held it a prisoner to earth's murky atmosphere, and rejoicing in its freedom.

I wish I could find words to express the ecstatic bliss of my freed spirit when I found that, like a glad sunbeam, I could move, at will, through regions of boundless space, should soon be able to visit the distant planets and fixed stars, which in the earth-life I had contemplated with so much wonder and admiration; rejoiced that I should soon know the secret of the sun's rising beams, the mission and origin of the comets; learn the mysteries and glories of the spirit world; and, oh, rapturous anticipations, behold the face of my dear Redeemer! "There, too, I shall find my beloved Lina!" I thought. "Oh, precious certainty! I shall clasp again her dear hands, hear once more her sweet voice, gaze into her loving eyes, aye, enjoy her companionship through all the cycling ages of eternity!"

After they had buried my body and left the cemetery I looked down through the moist earth with which they had covered my sleeping dust and wondered, as I saw the sunken eyes, faded cheeks and purple lips, how I could have wasted so much time in life, in decorating the form which must soon become food for the all-conquering worm; why I had been proud of "this corruptible which must soon put on corruption;" then, with as little pity for my cast-off body as I felt for the clods of earth which covered it, I flew away, rejoicing that it could no longer hold me earthward, and started on my ærial tour, singing:

" 'Happy the spirit released from its clay,
Happy the soul that goes bounding away.' "

Away, above the clouds, far, far beyond the upper blue, beyond the solar system, and other systems whose suns and centers are the fixed stars in the distant nebulæ, out into the wide silence and eternal midnight of illimitable space my happy spirit took its joyous flight in search of the shores of the hereafter, "The everlasting gardens."

Suddenly a light from the still distant heaven crept faintly into this "measureless void" through which I was still passing with the velocity of thought. It grew brighter each moment. Then music, sweet as distant startled the awful silences into life and melody. But the light increased in brilliancy, and the music grew more bewilderingly sweet as I approached the BEAU-

TIFUL CITY. "Am I, indeed, nearing the jasper and sapphire walls, and are those the pearly gates?" I cried, as they burst upon my vision. "And the gates are wide open, thanks be to Christ who giveth the victory! But—*shall I be permitted to enter?*"

The scene before me was glorious beyond description. Light, unearthly in its whiteness and brightness, more resplendant than the sunbeams, whiter than the glittering snow, appeared to radiate from some hidden source or centre. It seemed unlike anything terrestrial. As my vision became clearer I found myself in a lovely ante-chamber, and saw coming to meet me my seraphic Lina. She was robed in shining white. A halo of light encircled her head, but her face, which was far more beautiful than in life, wore the old, radiant smile of welcome. She was leading a little white-robed, golden-haired child, who seemed, at first, like the spirit of my own lost childhood, but one I soon recognized as my infant sister, Olive, who died before I was born.

No pen, or pencil, or human language is adequate to portray my unspeakable bliss at that moment. My soul flew to embrace them; but Lina beckoned me away, after pointing to a glorious Being just within the gates.

"It is my Saviour!" I cried. "Let me go to Him, my angel Lina."

"No, Mary," she answered. "The Father has not called you. You are needed upon the earth. Go back for a little while and wait patiently your appointed time. You will be called for soon." Then the gates were closed. No words of mine can express my disappointment. I was plunged at once from ecstatic joy to the deepest sorrow, but ere I had commenced my downward flight I awoke, and behold! it was ALL A DREAM!

CHAPTER XIX.

A DREAM OVER BRIDE CAKE.

Girls, did you ever dream over wedding cake? Well, I did, when I was a very young girl. Listen and I will tell you my dream. It occurred while I was a student at Wyoming Seminary, and was deeply interested in Grecian and Roman mythology, which study accounts for much that was horrifying in my vision.

Of course, I was a young and joyous bride roaming in dreamland with my long-dreamed-of Adonis. Hand in hand, we roamed through flowery groves in the balmy air of the Elysian Fields, whose cloudless sunshine, placid waters and amaranthine bowers filled our souls with joy unspeakable. We drank only the nectar which the gods love, and subsisted on celestial fruits and delicious bride cake; listened to the sweetest music, and enjoyed the aroma and beauty of the innumerable flowers, until Zeus suddenly appeared in his chariot of winged lightning, and, with a frown, dashed our cup of bliss to the earth! Then came the Fates and cut the Gordian knot which had bound us together, and in a moment the glory had departed and we were driven from the Elysian Fields by the Furies with whips of scorpions.

Thirst, intolerable thirst, burned our lips and throats and compelled us to quaff the deadening waters of the Lethe. Instantly all remembrance of our former joy vanished, and we sank down, down, into the dismal abode of Erebus, the dark-winged night.

Here a group of winged fiends bore my companion away and

the Furies, with their snaky curls, carried me to the shore of the loathsome river Styx, where I saw all the terrible shades of hunger, disease, old age, despair and death waiting for Charon and his leaky boat to row them over the river, beyond which we saw waves of lurid fire rolling slowly along the shore of Pluto's subterranean abode called Hades.

Oh! the agonies, the infinite tortures which seized me, as I entered the abode of the damned! Innumerable fiery serpents wreathed their burning coils around me, and I could see their red tongues and fiery eyes gleaming in the darkness as I sank down, down, into an abyss of liquid fire! The sulphurous flames were suffocating me, yet I could not die. Every moment (which seemed longer than I had imagined eternity to be) increased my torment, both mental and physical. Louder grew the groans of the lost, fiercer burned the sulphurous flames and more tightly coiled the burning serpents around me. I asked the dire Medusa how long I was thus doomed to suffer, and she answered: *"Forever and ever!"* and her words seemed to reverberate throughout the deep and measureless caverns of hell. At that moment a hideous demon, whose face I recognized as that of a murderer whom I had seen on earth, flew away with me into the subterranean depths, which were peopled with millions of lost spirits, and, with a shriek which aroused every girl in the dormitory, I awoke to find that it was all a dream, or "nightmare" vision. Girls, take my advice, and never again dream over bride cake.

CHAPTER XX.

THE HAUNTED CHAMBER.

In the year 1882 I made a tour of the oil regions and visited the cities of Northwestern Pennsylvania and the State of New York as far as Buffalo. My business was to establish agencies for my new book, just issued from the press, and also to place it in the book stores along the line. Somewhere in the heart of the Alleghenies I struck a small manufacturing city, surrounded by mountains and forests, but boasting of all the modern improvements, including electric lights and cars, natural gas for fuel, and the town, with its immense machine shops, run and lighted by electricity, the steel works constituting the chief industry of the wealthy little city.

It was hard to obtain board outside of the quiet hotels and boarding houses, but I finally did find a large front room in a private house, with excellent board at a reasonable figure. The house was large and stood back from the street in a lot filled with peach, apple and cherry trees, and my well-furnished and lighted room was on the second floor.

The first night, or rather, morning, I occupied it, it was 3 o'clock precisely, I was suddenly awakened from a pleasant dream of home by hearing the sound of a pair of scissors being dashed upon the floor in front of my bed. Thinking a burglar was in my room, I sprang out of bed, turned on the electric light and looked hurriedly around the apartment, but there was not a sign of a burglar or pair of scissors, or even a cat to be seen, while the doors leading to my quarters from the bath closet and hall were as securely locked as I had left them, before retiring.

For one month this first night's experience was repeated nightly. It was in vain that I searched for a movable panel in the wall, a trap door under the carpet, or secret passage from the closet or bath room to the hall, and the heavy inside window shutters were always securely fastened. No one could have entered over the transom, as it was too low.

I finally grew nervous and so sleepless that I spoke to my landlady. She was a young married woman, and had only resided there a month or two before my advent, and I was her first boarder. She laughed heartily at my "freak of imagination," as she called it, and advised me "to get a bottle of valerian," but finally declared that it was only the click of a gate next door. A fireman boarded there, and invariably took his train with her husband, who was an engineer, at 3 P. M. She always heard him open and shut the gate at that hour. "I often hear the sharp, metallic click of that gate," she added. "It closes automatically." (She was a graduate of a high school in Boston.)

This explanation partially quieted me and a few days later I resumed my itinerancy for another month. After a successful tour I arrived late one night and went immediately to my room at my former boarding place, and was soon fast asleep. I had almost forgotten the scissors episode, and was too tired to once think of it before retiring; but at precisely 3 A. M. the following morning, crash; went the ghostly scissors; and I was not only awakened, but frightened by the nearness to my bed of that metallic sound. Somehow this time it seemed to "get on my nerves," and I slept no more for two hours, when I fell asleep and dreamed that I saw a woman lying on my bed, sobbing wildly, while bending over her and seizing her hands with his left hand, I saw a man stab her three times with a pair of long, bright scissors, and awoke in terror, to find that it was all a cruel nightmare, but a dream so real that her screams seemed still to ring in my ears.

I hastily dressed, gathered up my few belongings, my baggage was still at the station, took a hasty breakfast, paid my astonished landlady, and hurried away for the early train, without explaining the cause of my sudden hegira.

A pleasant-faced young woman in the next seat to mine smiled and said:

"Good morning. I did not know that you had returned."

I recognized her as the clerk in the local book store, whom I had seen during my first visit to the city.

"I hope you are not leaving us for good," she added.

"But I am," I answered, with, I felt, a gruesome smile, as I looked back through a gap in the mountains at the fast receding city.

"Rather sudden, isn't your going? I heard you were to remain another month. When did you return?"

"Last night, on the midnight flyer."

She looked at me and smiled. "Did anything frighten or annoy you at your boarding house?" I did not answer, and she continued with a grimace:

"Was it *scissors?*"

"It was scissors," laconically, "but how did you hear? Did my nice landlady tell you?"

"Oh, no! But haven't you heard that that house is haunted?"

"No. Tell me all you know about it, please."

"Well, I will. The landlady is a stranger, and has only been here a short time, and you were her first boarder. Some years ago the man who owns the place, a rich owner of several steel mills, returned to England, leaving his mansion in charge of his agent, who allowed a dressmaker to move into it as caretaker. This caretaker had a daughter of perhaps sixteen, Mary Leon, who was considered very handsome, although a trifle fast, and altogether too fond of dress and jewelry. The girl had a lover— a Frenchman and a stranger—but, contrary to her mother's wish, persisted in keeping his company, although he was a dissipated gambler. One night her mother was found dead—murdered. She had been stabbed by a pair of scissors in the *front room of the second floor*—stabbed through the heart and lungs—but her daughter Mary and her lover, Count Imo, had disappeared.

"They had been seen leaving the house together early in the evening, dressed as if for a journey, and driving toward the station in a cab, and rumor said that they had eloped and gone to foreign parts; but from the night of the tragedy to the present nothing has been seen of them. It was known that Mrs. Leon had opposed her child's marriage; also, that all of Mrs. Leon's hard-earned money and jewelry were missing. A number of people have tried to live in that house, but have soon left, declaring that it is haunted by the dead woman and the pair of scissors by which she was murdered nine years ago. Now, do tell me what you heard, please."

I briefly told her and she promised not to spoil my hostess' honeymoon by telling her the story. And now for the sequel of the haunted chamber.

TWENTY YEARS LATER.

In the summer of 1903, twenty-one years later, I wrote my quandum friend, the pretty bookdealer of the mountain-rimmed electric city, asking if she had heard anything more about the scissors-haunted chamber where I had roomed in 1882, and she replied by the next eastgoing mail after receiving my letter; and by the way, reader, she is a fine narrator, and would be a credit to any class in elocution in the summer session of Columbia University, New York. She had been married ten years to the proprietor of the City Book Store, and was still its manager.

SEQUEL TO THE HAUNTED CHAMBER.

"Yes," she wrote, "the sequel to the 'Scissors Tragedy' has been solved. A year ago last March a sickly looking, half-famished woman of '45, though she looked ten years older, arrived on the midnight train from Buffalo. She was clad in a gown of gray outing flannel, with a long cape of the same, and wore a Tam-o'-Shanter hood of the same material. Her hair was gray and unkempt and her clothes soiled and ragged. She was blue with cold, but walked unsteadily into the ladies' waiting-room and fell fainting near the steam heater, and horrors! a bundle, which she had concealed under her cape, slid to the floor, and those present beheld the stiffened form and cold, white face of a dead child!

"A tender-hearted woman lifted the corpse and gently laid it on a nearby settee, crying: 'It has been dead for days! I saw her enter the railway carriage at Toronto, but never dreamed what was in the bundle she was carrying. See how emaciated the little girl's face and arms are! She must have died of starvation!'

"Yes, you have guessed correctly. The child's mother was Mary Leon, daughter of the murdered dressmaker of scissors fame. She recovered from her fainting fit and was conveyed to the emergency hospital, where she told the following story, amid sobs and tears, as she clung to the dead child, which she refused to allow any one to take away. She said, in part: 'My husband, Count Imo, was always cruel to me. He often beat me unmercifully because his meals were not ready, when there was nothing to eat in the house.

" 'We went to Canada, and he lived by his wits, fishing, hunting, gambling, prize fighting, *stealing*—for he was a natural thief—and spent years of his life in prison. Before we had been married a month I threatened to go back to my mother, but he showed me a newspaper from home, telling about my mother's murder by her daughter's lover, also implicating me, so I was afraid to go home. My children—there were five—have all died from want and the effects of their father's cruelty.'

" 'Why did he kill your mother?' was asked.

" 'I was in my room packing my valise, when I heard them quarreling. My mother sprang at him with a pair of scissors she had been using, and there was a struggle, he told me, in which she was stabbed through the heart while he was trying to gain possession of them. He had laid her on the bed, *flung the scissors on the floor,* and rushed through the hall, just as I was leaving my own room. He seized my valise and hurried me downstairs and into a carriage that was waiting, and we were married in Buffalo.

"'A week ago, after kicking and beating me, he flung my little Mazy on the floor so violently as to break her arm, and left the house in a fearful rage because I asked him for some money to buy food. He was killed later in the day by a vicious horse, and because I could not pay for his burial his body was sent to the college of anatomy in a distant city, I am glad to say.

"'I sold my few household goods to a neighbor for enough money to bring us home, but we have had no food since we started. My little girl died in my arms on the train the night I left Canada, but I kept her death a secret for fear they would take her from me. But I am starving! For the love of God, nurse, give me a cup of tea and piece of bread!' After eating and drinking ravenously, she sprang up and said: 'Now I must go home!' A policeman followed her and saw her go directly to the house where you boarded, and into the front chamber on the second floor, where her mother was murdered, and where you roomed, and lay her dead child upon the bed, just as the policeman appeared, when she gave a blood-curdling scream and tried to spring out of an open window. The little corpse received a decent burial—and the mother was sent to prison. She was tried for the murder of her mother, but a council of medical experts having pronounced her incurably insane, she was acquitted. From that day to this Mary Leon Imo has been an incurable paranoiac in the State Lunatic Asylum.

The house where you boarded has been sold to a syndicate of city physicians for a sanitarium, and that chamber on the second floor is a consulting office and operating room. Thus endeth the story of the Haunted Chamber, for if the murdered lady walks there still at night, there is no one there to hear; but the strangest part of it all is, that the young couple had been to a ball the night of the murder and only reached the Leon home about 2 A. M. They took the 3.20 train for Buffalo, consequently the murder was committed about 3 o'clock.

"Perhaps the dead woman's spirit returned nightly to induce some one to ferret out the mystery and bring the murderer to justice.

"Or, it may be that she was worrying about her daughter, and was desirous of effecting her rescue from the knave who had lured her to her ruin. Alas! We shall never in this life be able to elucidate the mystery.

" 'But there are more things in heaven and earth, Horatio,
 Than were dreamt of in your philosophy.'

"Your whilom landlady moved away about the first of January because the house had been sold. I think they are living in Buffalo."

CHAPTER XXI.

THE MYSTERY OF RIVERFORD.

THAT "All good things come to those who wait," is not always apparently true, yet I believe that a majority of mysterious happenings will be solved if we wait long enough and seek their solution patiently and perseveringly.

Over thirty years ago I took passage in a small steamboat on a well-known river, *en route* for a certain village twenty-five miles distant, where I had accepted a situation as teacher during my college vacation. We arrived at Riverford about midnight, where I was to take a stage for S——, ten miles distant, but, as the boat was several hours behind schedule time, I was obliged to spend the remainder of the night at Riverford Hotel. A boy of sixteen, whom I had found in the office, escorted me into the old stone tavern, and, after passing through several dreary-looking rooms on the lower floor, led me into a long, lone, wainscotted apartment, which overlooked a canal, and said, as he went peering into dark corners and under the bed and chairs:

"I don't see any rattlesnakes, but they do creep in here sometimes through them cracks in the wall, Miss," lighted a tallow candle and left me alone in the semi-gloom of my bedroom. There was no way to fasten my door, as the lock had been removed, but I was too weary for fear, and soon slept; but while an old, wheezy clock in the hall was striking one I was awakened by a terrible scream in a woman's voice; then, as I sprang out of bed, these words: "Good God Almighty! Murder! Murder! Help! Edward! Help! Help!!"

The noise was in the chamber above, and light streamed through crevices in the broken ceiling overhead.

Then footsteps seemed to approach hastily, and a struggle was plainly heard amid curses and cries, which almost drove me mad; then all was still, except the sound of dragging a heavy body over the chamber floor.

Of course, I was out of bed and dressed in less time than it takes to write it, but when I approached the outside door a huge mastiff disputed my right of exit and I was a prisoner in the old stone tavern, for both of my windows overlooked the river, or canal, and were strongly fastened. Imagine my fright! I was only a young, timid girl, just out of school, and my heart seemed to stand still. That they would murder me next I felt certain.

I remember dragging the heavy bedstead against the door, then hiding my hat and traveling bag between the two mattresses, and of creeping after them, hoping thus to make the robbers or murderers think that I had escaped; for I had smoothed the bed and pillows and extinguished my light, and was about falling into sleep, when I suddenly remembered that they would know I was still there because *my bedstead was against the door.* I remained there, however, for three mortal hours, scarcely daring to breathe; but when the clock struck four I crept out of bed, seized hat and bag and ran to the old-fashioned looking-glass to see if my hair had turned white in a single night, like that of the poor, unfortunate French queen of historical fame; but, to my surprise, it had not become gray during that terrible night.

"Thank God, it is daylight!" I whispered, as I made my way

out of doors. The office boy was still in the dingy little office. To my inquiries, he told me the way to the nearest town, where I could take the stage for S——, but seemed surprised at my haste. "You will have plenty of time for breakfast before stage time, and it is a mile to S——," he said, and, as I paid for my lodging and gave directions about having my trunk sent by the stage, asked:

"Say, Miss, didn't you sleep good? Did anything scare you last night?"

"Why do you ask me?" was my answer, for I was afraid to tell him.

"Because, your eyes look so big and wide-awake—I was afraid you had seen or heard one of them rattlers," with a comical wink, which enlightened me as to the snake business, and I hurried away, smiling in spite of myself, knowing that the young wag had been trying to frighten me.

On my way to S—— I decided not to tell any one about my frightful experience, for, that a murder had been committed I had not the slightest doubt, and I might easily be arrested as an accessory after the fact if I made a confidante of the public.

My destination was reached in safety, and, after a successful summer, I returned to college by railroad, instead of steamboat, and for nearly thirty years my secret remained my own, when once more I had occasion to visit the town of S——, but I went by train, and again lived over, in memory that night of horror, in the old stone tavern.

A middle-aged lady entered the car at Riverford station and took the vacant chair beside me, and when a mile further down the noble, elm-shaded river we passed a dilapidated stone house,

I asked her if she knew the family that had occupied it in 1873, she replied that she had been acquainted with the family all her life—that only one of them—Edward—was living. That splendid mansion on the hill yonder is his summer residence, but he is a Congressman now and spends his winters in Washington, D. C. John, his brother, died of delirium tremens in 1873, in the early autumn, thirty years ago, I think. He drank heavily for years, and the spring before his death tried while in a fit of delirium tremens to murder his sister by choking her to death in the dead of the night. And he would have killed her but for the timely appearance of his brother Edward. As it was, he choked her into insensibility, and she never recovered from the shock to her nervous system. He died at an inebriate's home a few months later. His brother does not drink and is a very popular politician. The story of John's attempted murder was kept secret until after his death. The homestead has been deserted for many years." She left at the next station, and I could not help saying to myself "Eureka! After thirty years the Mystery of Riverside has been solved satisfactorily!"

"But," you say, dear reader, "if you had not have been so insanely frightened and had remained long enough to make inquiries you would have found out the mystery thirty years earlier."

"Oh, yes—true—but the reason why I relate this story here is to prove that many mysterious occurrences, both in the world of metaphysics and real life, may be explained to our entire satisfaction, if we only *wait long enongh,* or search long enough, to find a solution, or to unravel the mystery."

CHAPTER XXII.

ELUCIDATION.

In my childhood I was not inclined to be very superstitious. I remember, also, that I was in the habit of investigating everything that appeared unnatural. On my way to school I had to pass an extensive cemetery, and used to hurry past it, like other children. One evening, as I was returning from church alone, I heard footsteps, as usual, behind me. My whole soul seemed to be in a listening mood, and I soon found that the steps kept pace with my own. I stopped short. The pursuing feet stopped, too. I started again and so did my phantom pursuer. "It is only the echo of my own footsteps!" I exclaimed, and went on my way rejoicing. That graveyard was divested of its terrors ever afterward.

At another time, when spirit rappings were being heard by many people in almost every town, I was awakened one night by a singular tapping on my bedroom wall. After listening to the weird sound for hours in the dead of the night, I concluded that at last I was visited by the wonderful spirit rappings. I had read how to spell by the "raps" and began to ask questions of my spiritual visitant. They were answered to my entire satisfaction and I concluded, before dawn, that I, too, was to be a great medium. Daylight found me, however, in a more dubious mood. "I will search everywhere *outside* and inside of my room before mentioning my experience to the family," I said. After satisfying myself that there was nothing in my bedroom which could produce the singular "thud," "thud," which still continued at intervals, I opened my window and looked cautiously around. The mystery was soon solved. An old goose was sitting close to the wall under my window, pecking away at the clap-boards in the most methodical manner. She was dreaming of picking grass, or else imagined that she was down in the pasture, for she kept up a ceaseless pick, pick, pick, at the wood, notwithstanding my laughter. I should have been a medium, in all human probability, but for this habit of investigating every unusual sound or appearance which frightened me in my childhood.*

There are some mysteries which cannot be explained. The same answer, I think, may be given about supernatural appearances before the death of a friend—they may be optical illusions.

Mysterious sounds may often be accounted for by natural causes—the settling of walls, or timbers, or foundations of a house, caused by frost, heat, or moisture, for instance. But how explain the ringing of bells by unseen hands, or the playing of the piano by the *"Invisible Musician?"* It was not imagination in either case, or in the case of the "Haunted Chamber." For this was heard by too many witnesses, and the last too often to be explained in this way; but although not in the same category, *The Mystery at Riverford* was explained later in a most satisfactory manner to the narrator, after the expiration of three decades, as I have stated already.

*It is a pity I did not keep up this habit in after years.

Startling impressions may, on the principle of mental telepathy, or of brain waves, have been sent to us from friends thousands of miles away, instead of from the spirit world. For it is the opinion of many scientists that friends at a distance can influence each other's minds by persistently thinking of each other, or by earnestly desiring to see or hear from one another by letter. Else why are we often writing to our correspondents at the very time they are writing to us? Or thinking of a friend and wishing to see her the very moment she is on her way to visit us, her plans all unknown to ourselves?

But what about dreams fulfilled? Sometimes the fear of a future catastrophe, or death, or the desire for some event of importance to transpire, has caused the *dream*, but not its fulfilment. The mind is never dormant, even in sleep, and we have had a thousand dreams which were not remembered and were never fulfilled. "But dreams, and visions, and prophesies were often sent to people in old Bible days," you say, "and if so, why not in our day?" May I reply, "Because we have no open vision." In a recent study of the Scriptures I found to my astonishment that almost all of the important events narrated in the Bible were foreshadowed by dreams, visions and prophesy.

"But," you still ask, "what about dreams and impressions as monitions?" Here I am obliged to confess that I believe these prophetic dreams and sudden impulses as well as lightning flash impressions do seem to have been sent as warnings, or to prepare us for the coming wave of sorrow which is about to sweep over our souls like an overwhelming deluge. "Well, what about strange appearances—ghostly visitants?"

I copied the following from a well-known work on psychology:

"A certain judge, with his wife, were stopping at a hotel in a neighboring city. The lady was an invalid and suffered greatly from insomnia. She complained to her husband morning after morning that their chamber was haunted. That she saw, every night, a woman knitting near the foot of her bed. At first the judge laughed at her, called her fanciful or nervous; but, in order to convince him, she awoke him one night and whispered: 'Look! There she is again!' The incredulous judge had to acknowledge that his wife was right, but after looking at the busy knitter a few minutes, arose and went to the window, near the foot of the bed, and found a small rent in the curtain. Placing his eye at the spot, he saw in a room across the street a woman knitting industriously. There was a lamp near her and over her head was suspended a pair of concave mirrors, which had reflected her image and flung it into the chamber across the way. The judge called his wife to the window, and was rewarded for his trouble by hearing her laugh heartily, and declare that she would seek out the nocturnal knitter and give her pecuniary aid on the morrow.

Reflection and refraction of the rays of light will account for many spectral visitants."

Do you ask, reader mine, if they will account for all such apparitions? I cannot tell. The Sacred Book says that King Saul saw Samuel's spirit after the *prophet had been dead five years,* also that Moses 1490 years after his death, and Elias 950 years after death, appeared to Jesus when he was transfigured on the mountain and talked with him; and were seen by Peter, James and John.

Then, why may not our friends revisit us of the earth, do you still ask? I must again take refuge in agnosticism—I do not know. Yet I am not an agnostic. The *Phrenological Journal* of December, 1878, says, in an article entitled "Brain and Mind:" "Marvelousness in its relation to the spiritual elements of the human character, prompts to belief in the supernatural and religious. Dr. Gall was led to the discovery of this organ by observing that some individuals imagine themselves to be visited by apparitions of persons dead or absent, and the question occurred to him: 'How does it happen that men of considerable intellect often believe in the reality of ghosts and visions? Or, is there a particular organ which imposes, in this form, upon the human understanding? And how are such illusions explained? He studied the history of those remarkable for this quality of mind, and, in comparing their busts and pictures, his attention was drawn to a fullness existing in the region of the head now allotted to this faculty. Following up the matter, he examined the heads of people known for uncommon credulity wherever they fell in his way, and finally concluded upon the location and function of the organ called *marvelousness*. Socrates, as every classical scholar knows, believed that he was attended by a spirit which served him as a guide. Joan of Arc believed she had a communication from God through St. Michael, who appeared to her and made known His will in regard to France. Tasso often held conversations with familiar spirits as with companions of flesh and blood. Swedenbourg says: 'In 1743 it pleased the Lord to manifest Himself to me, and to appear personally before me, to give me a knowledge of the spiritual world, and to place me in communication with angels and spirits, and this power has been continued with me until the present day.

* * *' The development of marvelousness is very marked in this distinguished man. Napoleon believed in his 'star of destiny,' and set much store by lucky days. It is unreasonable to suppose that in these cases and in very many others which might be mentioned, these visions and supernatural appearances are mere vagaries of imagination. They are as real to such individuals as hues and tints of flowers and the harmony of sounds are to the majority of mankind, although, to be sure, there are some people color-blind, who can form no idea of color, and some deaf, to whom music can have no charm. The explanation which phrenology gives to these cases of preternatural impressions is that man is endowed with a mental organ called marvelousness in phrenology, which, in its normal activity, produces a love of the new and wonderful, and disposes to a belief in the actual presence of supernatural beings.

"In the London Bedlam Mr. Combe examined the head of a patient in whom this organ was largely developed, and whose insanity consisted in seeing phantoms and being led to act as if they were realities. In the Richmond Lunatic Asylum, at Dublin, he saw several patients in whom this organ predominated, and whose insanity consisted in believing themselves supernatural beings or inspired. * * *

"Persons who have exhibited extraordinary zeal in the propagation of some religious sect or doctrine, like De Sales, Loyola, Whitefield, Jacob Boehem, or Ann Lee, show in their portraits a large endowment of marvelousness or spirituality. In the casts or portraits of Thomas Paine, Voltaire, Cardinal de Retz, the organ is very deficient."

The most intellectual New Englanders believed in witchcraft

a century ago. To-day only the most ignorant believe in witches. So it will be with spiritualism, clairvoyance, hypnotism, one hundred years to come, in all probability, under the white searchlight of scientific research.

In regard to the so-called *"Second Sight,"* the scientists are still utterly unable to account for it, or to explain it, except from a psychological and phrenological view, namely, that some individuals are endowed with a larger organ of marvelousness than others, causing them to have warnings of death or coming disaster.

I found in a treatise entitled *Popular Superstitions,* published by Allen & Ticknor, Boston, Mass., in 1832, that the writer accounted for "the superstitious fear of ghosts in crossing a graveyard at midnight as the outcome of silly parents' and foolish nursemaids' talks to children. Telling them ghost stories before going to bed, or that "the ghosts will get them if they do not go to sleep," will give rise to a shuddering fear which will follow them through life. The belief in witchcraft was once universal throughout the civilized world.

"It is now believed only by a few ignorant people. We should make the love and fear of God the true basis of our education."

To-day very few believe in astrology, while fortune-telling and palmistry are believed in by few, except the gypsies.

Do you ask: "How do you account for that Spirit Telegram?" If we have guardian angels, perhaps it came from one of them. Or, perhaps, my brother's dying thoughts influenced mine (although I was 1,500 miles away) by a brain wave or wireless telegram—telepathy—call it what you please.

"But how explain the appearance of ghostly visitants?" I

cannot explain them, because I do not know whether they are real visions or evanescent dreams between sleeping or waking, or caused by the sudden recollection or reappearance of some forgotten story told to me in childhood, which had been, at that early age, painted indelibly on my inner vision or consciousness.

We have inherited superstitious tendencies and an uncontrollable fear of death from a long line of superstitious ancestors. but the fear of ghosts and hobgoblins has, in a majority of cases, if not in all, been *acquired*. *It is a habit.*

As I have already quoted, the habit of telling ghost stories to a little child at bedtime by her nurse or ignorant mother, is a crime which cannot be condoned, for the creeping horror which the child experiences will never be forgotten. Therefore, psychologists and phrenologists are correct in their belief that parents and nursery-maids are responsible for the fear of ghosts, and have been for many ages. "The habit," says the above-mentioned writer, "of governing young children by *fear,* is a most pernicious one, and is accountable for their fear in the dark and the vein of superstition which will follow till their dying day, causing them to see visions and dream dreams which to them appear real, but which, in reality, are only pictures of long-forgotten tales, which some sudden awakening of memory has brought up from quiescent or dormant brain cells, and rehabilitated in the forms and features of their own lost friends."

But what of dreams of death or disaster, or how do you account for dreams fulfilled, you still ask.

Alexander Wilder says: "The night-time of the body is the day-time of the soul. In sleep the soul is freed from the constraint of the body, and enters upon the life of highest intelligence," and, although I am willing, in my story entitled *"What Was It?"* to affirm that I did not believe I had slept, still it is possible that I did lose consciousness for a moment, or, perhaps, my own fearful thoughts and the memory of his sufferings may have conjured up the well-remembered picture of the sufferer, which was photographed on the retina of my mind's eye. "But, does this explain 'Who Was It,' or the brother's and sister's similar vision of the dead Eulalie?" do you still ask. Could it have been some former servant or pretty kleptomaniac, who had let herself in with a duplicate key, and taken free lodging in the deserted house for the winter? Did she hide within the ample folds of a cloak, or gown in the wardrobe or in a locker, or was it an optical illusion painted by memory and fancy? Deponent does not know.

There have been witches, wizards, sorcerers, soothsayers, in all ages. In our day spiritualism, hypnotism, clairvoyance and belief in dreams and omens continue to feed the imagination and foster the growth of superstition.

Possibly, science will yet explain all the mysteries which have puzzled the learned and ignorant alike for six thousand years, nearly; but do we not attach too much importance to ghost-lore mysticisms? Are there not mysteries all about us equally as great which science has failed to elucidate? How do plants grow? How do they know when to blossom? Why are there several different shades and colors in the same class and family of flowers in the same bed and under the same sun and state of cultivation? Do you tell me that the colors come from the acids and alkalies in said plants or soil? All right, but how do you prove the truth of your assertion? Can you tell me how plants know when to close and when to open? Can you cheat a night-blooming cereus by electric light, or by darkening the room sufficiently to cause it to blossom by daylight? Can you make a century plant bloom before its time by cultivation?

A word further about startling impressions. Listen well to these *Tongueless Voices,* for they may have been sent by your guardian angel from a higher intelligence; perhaps they are the voice of God speaking to the soul.

Yes, I still believe in guardian angels, dear reader, and shall until my dying day.

The only disgraceful period in our country's early history was that of the Salem Witchcraft, and those strange illusions still remain unexplained.

It is sad and almost incredible that we shall be afraid to be alone with our dearest and nearest friends *as soon as they are dead,* but such will be the case with us all, although we laugh at the idea, now, of such superstitious nonsense. May not this also be ascribed to our early instruction? I mean the dread of staying alone with a corpse. Yet, in a great battle, soldiers become so inured to death that they often build barricades of *dead bodies* and handle them with as little feeling as they would logs or sand bags.

So it will be in future with children and older individuals. As the races of mankind progress in enlightenment and religion, their fear of the dead and the supernatural will lose its horrors.

And it may be that, in the glorious age to come, they will not only welcome spirit telegrams, sent from the other world by angels, as calmly as we now read accounts of wireless telegrams, and ghostlore will have no more terrors for the children and young people of the future than the history of Salem witchcraft has for us, who are living in the dawn of the twentieth century, or than fairy tales have for the children of to-day.

I like the closing thought in *Popular Superstitions:* "We should make the love and fear of God the true basis of our education."

The more we study the life and character of Jesus Christ, the more we shall admire his majestic dignity, self-poise and absence of weakness in all trying situations. He talked as calmly with angels and resurrected spirits as with his desciples; spoke as composedly with the legion of devils at Gadara and with Beelzebub in the wilderness, and on the high mountain, and with as much fearlessness as if he were speaking to Martha and Mary and His friend Lazarus; for even the evil spirits respected the Divine Master. If we ask Him to deliver us from evil He will heed our prayers.

In closing this chapter, allow me to repeat, the lesson I would teach is this: Never tell ghost stories or tales of witchcraft, or mention the spectral illusions witnessed by yourself or friends to young children, because these weird tales will, as has been said in these pages, remain in brain cells for years, then suddenly appear in the form of spectral illusions.

Many of these so-called *apparitions,* as I have already told you, have been traced back to stories told in childhood or some pictured face of a long-dead ancestor, which was exhibited to us in our early years by some aged grandmother.

I would also tell little children that a so-called ghost is the most harmless thing imaginable. That it is merely a spiritual body which can pass through bolted and locked doors just as our thoughts can pass through solid walls or closed doors, without touching or injuring the inmates in the rooms through which they pass. That they are as harmless as the shadows which we see all around us, and I would read to them Luke xxiv. 39th verse, John xx., 19-26.

I would teach them to be kind to the living, but to have no fear of the dead.

THE END.

www.ingramcontent.com/pod-product-compliance
Lightning Source LLC
LaVergne TN
LVHW011203080426
835508LV00007B/582